T0013946

For my mum, Fay Barratt.
Because you have always trusted me.

Tinder
Translator

An A–Z
of Modern
Misogyny

Aileen Barratt

Hardie Grant

BOOKS

Contents

Introduction

"Tinder is the worst, and yet here we are."

—*Me, in my Tinder bio*

We may be well into the 21st century, but misogyny is very much alive and well. Nowhere is this more apparent than in the world of dating apps. Anyone who presents as a woman will have encountered sexism in their everyday life of course, but the way a lot of men speak to women on Tinder (or Bumble or Hinge or whichever new app has launched since I wrote this intro) is different from how they speak to women in person. And by different, I mean worse.

When I first heard about dating apps, I had no use for them. Tinder was launched in 2012, a time when I was 27, happily married and highly smug. The idea of swiping left and right on people's photos as a way of finding love (or whatever) was wild to me. I thought it was super shallow, looking through a directory of faces and deciding which ones you fancied and which you didn't almost instantly. Never mind that this is effectively the same thing I did in nightclubs on every night out of my single life. I remember saying the actual words 'Tinder is everything that is wrong with the world' more than once.

I know, I must have been unbearable.

Of course I, like most people, had no idea how much of an impact this one little app – and all those that came after it – would have. Before the dawn of smartphones (that's just normal phones to Gen Z) and dating apps, online dating was more of a niche pursuit. It was something gently suggested to the perpetually single: 'Have you thought about trying online?' Dating sites like Match and OKCupid were seen as the internet extension of lonely hearts pages in newspapers (ask your parents). Although these platforms grew in popularity throughout the late '90s and '00s, it wasn't until we could swipe left or right from the comfort of our own phone that online dating became the default for daters everywhere.

So, cut to four years later. Tinder is now the norm, the dating landscape has changed drastically, and my marriage has broken down. It was really shit, I was suddenly single, and I downloaded Tinder within three months (this is not a course of action I'd recommend to any newly separated person, but it's what I did).

Actually using dating apps hardly changed my attitude to them. I still thought they were pretty much the worst, hence the line in my Tinder bio. I just went from being smugly judgemental to reluctantly resigned. There's fun to be had, but fucking hell you have to wade through a lot of crap, especially if you are mainly swiping on cishet men.

Online, men seemed much more willing to talk to me as if I were an object, or to belittle me. It was impossible to escape how quickly half of them turned the conversation to sex. Not in a subtle, suggestive way either. There is nothing sexy about the way these men approach sex. It usually goes something like:

Step 1) Exchange pleasantries.
Step 2) Make a graphic sexual proposition or reference.
And it's not uncommon to skip step one.

We become hardened (pardon the pun) to the objectification and sleaze pretty quickly. Like most women, I built up a folder of screenshots of these kinds of interactions, whatsapping them to friends so we could all giggle and gag over the audacity and ickiness of these dudes.

It's not that I think online dating turned these men more sexist, just that the relative anonymity unmasks their misogyny. I suppose it's like any form of social media, where people are emboldened to be vitriolic in a way they probably couldn't muster in person. But it seems to go a step further with dating apps – the sheer volume of men being completely inappropriate is wild.

'On a dating site, you can act on impulses you might otherwise keep quiet,' says Christian Rudder in his 2014 book *Dataclysm*. 'The site doesn't connect to your family. Nothing gets posted to your friends' timelines … In a digital world that's otherwise compulsively networked, there's an old school solitude to online dating.'

Here Rudder is talking about the dating website he founded, OKCupid, but his observations definitely apply to the apps too. I'd argue the main difference between old-school dating sites and the apps is the scale on which they are used. That, and an increased focus on matching based solely on appearance (this was the aspect that outraged my smug 27-year-old self after all).

The scale has an impact because we begin to see each other as ever-replaceable; there is always another face to swipe on, another date to go on. This, coupled with the image-based nature of the apps (as opposed to dating sites, which generally ask people to fill in a lot more information about themselves), is a heady mix for your garden-variety misogynist. Add on the relative anonymity and it's like someone invented a way to streamline the objectification of women. Fun.

Of course, the lack of constant outside observation that online dating offers can be freeing, but it can also enable a lot of bullshit. Free from the constraints of public opinion, men who hold misogynistic views (and sadly that's a lot of them) can do as they like. It doesn't help that there are little to no consequences for sexualised pestering, or even throwing insults around as a way of coping with rejection, in these spaces.

There are some dating app behaviours that are pretty obviously misogynistic, but the subtler stuff takes longer to notice. It's often hidden in the repetitive, pithy statements that dating app bios are full of. 'Looking for someone who doesn't take themselves too seriously' and 'no drama' are two absolute classic stock phrases. They're so commonplace that after a while you stop thinking about them and what they actually mean. Even if what they mean is 'I hate women but I'd like to do sex'.

Every bio, however generic, has a subtext.

My Instagram page @TinderTranslators began as somewhere I would 'translate' awful bios I found into non-dating-app speak. It was a cathartic way for me to read douchebags for filth, and it made coming across several soul-destroyingly awful bios a day a bit more bearable – at least they were good content!

Soon, other women (and the occasional man) started sending me awful bios to translate. It doesn't seem to matter if you're in Manchester or Melbourne, the same stock phrases abound.

What I soon realised is that these phrases provided a way to talk about so much more than just Tinder. They gave me a jumping-off point to talk about how misogyny plays out in the world at large and especially in our personal relationships.

They started conversations about how men treat women and why we often don't expect more for ourselves.

The general fuckery of men, something that is enabled and exposed by the immediacy of dating app culture, has led to a pretty low bar for what generally constitutes a 'good guy'. There are so many arrogant dudebros talking over us about their favourite novelist (literally always a white American man from the 20th century), or creeps sending us dick pics, that when a man listens to us for more than a minute and, you know, doesn't sexually harass us, we immediately think he's a dreamboat.

Seriously, the bar is currently melting somewhere near the Earth's core. And there it will remain until men aren't applauded for extending us the most basic human courtesy.

Still, when you're wading through the quagmire of shite that is modern dating, sometimes it can be hard to see these things for yourself. What you need is some perspective. What you need is a girlfriend who will tell it like it is. A bit ranty, a bit sweary, she won't let you off the hook but she sure as hell won't let you sell yourself short either. She knows your worth and she'll be damned if you don't know it too.

Well, not to brag, but she is me. I am here to break down the bullshit in a handy A–Z guide. I want to interpret this language for you, and decode all of the sexist, and sometimes sinister, undertones that can be easy to miss.

This little collection of translations covers many phrases any dating app user will be all too familiar with, and a few that tend to come up once dating in person commences. Each chapter uses the stock phrase as a starting point to talk about the wider experiences of womanhood in a sexist world. You'll find quotes, notes and statistics dotted around, as well as a TL;DR (too long; didn't read) one-sentence summary at the end of every chapter. Modern dating culture has normalised a lot of crap that women shouldn't have to put up with, and we're not going to take it anymore, okay? We're going to raise the bar.

Before we begin

Just as there are stock phrases in the world of dating apps, there are also plenty of stock responses to my feminist readings of them. So, before we proceed into our A–Z tour of douchebaggery, I wanted to clear up a few things.

The 'not all' is implied

I may, at times, make some sweeping generalisations about men in this book. In fact I will. And if you're a man reading this (welcome, enjoy) you may sometimes think 'NOT ALL MEN'. So, in advance, let me tell you this – when I'm talking about men, the 'not all' is implied. I know men aren't a monolith, but they are a social group who hold privileges that certainly are generalisable.

I like some men a lot, in case you were wondering. So chill out. (Also, don't say 'not all men' out loud, it's super cringe, dude.)

Women do this too

A companion piece to 'not all men' is the shocking sentiment that women also behave badly.

On my Instagram page I often get the comment 'women do this too'. For example, I'll write about men who write 'NO DRAMA' in their bios and some helpful chap will inform me that women also include that in their profiles. Most of the dating app phrases I discuss in this book are also used by women. As a feminist, I fully accept that women can be dickheads. We are just as capable as men of being ego-driven pricks. Well, maybe not quite.

But, also as a feminist, I understand that the playing field of heterosexual dating is not even because we live in a patriarchy. There is a power imbalance that means that even if men and women use the same words, there are gendered dynamics that mean both the implications and the impact of those words can be vastly different.

So, when I talk about cishet men who write 'NO DRAMA' in their profiles, it is not me implying that women never say this. It's me talking about what it means when these men say it about women. We cool?

Please mind the binary

Gender isn't binary, but unfortunately misogyny is. Hatred of women – which is so woven into society that it is often undetectable – depends upon the idea that there are men and there are women and the former are superior to the latter. This is, to use a technical term, utter bullshit.

Not everyone exists inside of the gender binary. However, it is difficult to write a book about dating cishet men, especially misogynist ones, without employing binary language. All that is to say, if your gender is outside of the binary, you are valid and you are welcome here. Take what you can from this book; I hope there's lots for everyone.

Equally, this book speaks mostly to heterosexual dating. Again, the fact that love and sex can be enjoyed and reciprocated between all genders is a spanner in the works of the patriarchy. Misogynists almost always have vile homophobic views alongside their sexist ones, and queer folks have to navigate the world with similar vigilance to cishet women, always steeling themselves against potential attacks in all forms.

Dating in a queer context, however, doesn't mean you escape the bullshit of misogyny; just ask bisexual women! Whatever your sexuality, and if you're still working it out, I'm sure you will recognise much of the shite that comes up throughout.

To trans men and women

This book is about dating and misogyny, so necessarily I talk a lot about men and women in it! Trans men are men and trans women are women, that's not a subject that's up for debate.

When I talk about women, I am always including trans women. The only exception to this is when I refer to anatomy like the clitoris. Not all women have vulvas, but I do hope this book will have something to offer all women.

In my discussions of men here, I am largely talking about cisgender men. In my understanding, trans men often have a very different relationship with their masculinity – and that is generally a less toxic, more compassionate one. We can all harbour misogyny, no matter our gender, but cis men do seem to have that market cornered.

While not wanting to exclude anyone in writing this book, the idea that I could somehow encompass the lived experience of trans folks, when I am not and have never dated anyone trans, seems ignorant and misguided.

In short trans men are men, but I won't lump you in with the cis dudes in this context.

This is not a universal guide, obvs

I am one person who has read about and listened to the experiences of a bunch of other people. As with any writer, my experiences are often specific to my identity. I try as much as possible to disrupt that lens, to see my privileges and how they affect my experiences, but I can never fully step outside of myself.

I am white, cis and middle class. I grew up in a single-parent household. I am queer but I have only ever dated cishet men. I have a recurrent mental illness. I am non-disabled. I've been married and divorced. I have a child. All of these things add to the lens through which I see the world.

This book will resonate in parts and clang in others for anyone who has a different set of lived experiences than me. I have attempted to weave an understanding of this intersectionality into my writing, but from the outset I'd rather admit my limitations than over-reach in a doomed attempt at universality. A thousand performative caveats won't change the fact that everyone is always writing subjectively, and as long as we acknowledge this rather than try to assert our own experience of the world as the default, I think we'll be okay.

is for
Ask

"Just ask."

Translation: From the outset, I require that you make all the effort in this relationship.

'Just ask': never have so many told on themselves
so much with so few words.

Whenever I see 'just ask' in a bio, my immediate
reaction is: ask what? *Everything?* Why would I want
to spend that time and energy on someone who can't
think of three interesting things to say about
themselves? Or one, for that matter.

As anyone who has been on a dating app for more than five minutes will know, this charming two-worded bio is more common than it should be. Still, it's pretty useful in one way. Because it tells us all we need to know about the person who's written it: that they cannot be bothered and, crucially, that they think you should be. After all, A is also for audacity.

The longer form version of this bio often goes something like, 'I never know what to put here, so just ask me what you want to know.'

Well, Aaron, what if I want to know whether you have some kind of sense of self? What if I want to know if the person I'm potentially going to date is willing to spend more than half a second considering how they might want to come across? What if I don't want to begin a romantic encounter by doing all of the work?

I would bet money that Aaron would not take kindly to me 'just asking' any of these questions.

In fact, let's talk about the whole 'I never know what to write here' line, because it's such a non-statement. As far as I'm aware, no one *likes* writing bios. The rest of us aren't sitting down thinking, *Yay! Time to encapsulate my whole personality into five sentences in a way that will hopefully entice someone to think I'm attractive/funny/the potential love of their life, no pressure!*

Just like job applications, talking yourself up for strangers on the internet is weird and cringe. But, again like job applications, it's also necessary. If your CV said 'just ask', I'm pretty sure any potential employer would throw it in the bin while muttering 'arrogant twat' under their breath. But just-askers won't do their potential dates the courtesy of offering something, really just *any fucking thing*, that might be a selling point.

Unless, and hear me out here, that's because they don't have any selling points. It's a distinct possibility.

I have no proof of this, but I strongly suspect that the same people who write 'just ask' in their bio are the ones who complain that people on dating apps have 'no chat'. They probably roll their eyes when a match opens with 'hey' or 'how's your week?' But *what else are we supposed to say when you've given us nothing to go on, Anthony?* There has to be some give and take, mate. Which is why, for me, 'just ask' is an instant no. Because it gives nothing. There is a sort of energy-miser vibe to it. Like this person wants to put in minimum effort for maximum reward (aka a shag). And we are all worth more than minimum effort. You are worth more than minimum effort.

The word 'thoughtless' also comes to mind with this kind of bio. I'm pretty sure that most people who use it haven't thought very deeply about what they want from dating, or who they'd like to attract. I often get comments under the inane bios I share on Instagram saying something like 'do they really think this is going to work?' My reply is almost always the same – no, they don't think at all.

Because what is the alternative explanation? That they have thought it all through and have a deep confidence in the allure of their four poorly lit photos? That they think those two selfies, one group shot of the lads and one pic holding a big fish will spark such intrigue within us that we'll be simply bursting with enthusiastic questions we can't wait to 'just ask'? Surely no one sits down and constructs a well-thought-out plan of seduction that includes writing 'just ask' in their Tinder bio?

Perhaps a few people actually do use this phrase because they think it shrouds them in some sort of sexy mystery. If that's you then – and I mean this in the most loving way possible – stop it. There is no intrigue or allure in a two-worded instruction from a stranger. Only entitlement and mediocrity. In fact, those who are 'mysterious' about themselves on dating apps provoke suspicion in me more than anything else (see M is for Married for more on this subject).

Maybe you think I'm going too hard on the just-askers. Because **at least** they've written something. But honestly, I prefer no bio to this one. Blank bios are incredibly frustrating, but they don't ask anything of you. In contrast, 'just ask' is both the absence of a bio and the presence of a (albeit pretty passive) demand. No thanks.

A note on 'at least'

Because dating apps are often little more than quagmires of mediocrity and filth, our instinct can be to give credit where it's not even slightly due. Nowhere is this more apparent than in 'at least' sentences. *At least they're honest* (when stating that they have a pregnant girlfriend and are looking for 'fun'). *At least they reply* (monosyllabically with no follow-up questions). *At least they wrote something* (the something that they wrote was 'just ask'). If you catch yourself saying 'at least' about a potential match, listen. You are not here for the least. The least does not get credit. We deserve more.

If the just-askers can't make the effort to write a handful of sentences about themselves in order to get a date, what are they going to be like once they're on one? Are they going to ask us questions too? Pick a fun first-date activity? Engage with us on a human level in any way at all? Call me a cynic (because I am one) but I reckon the answer to all of those questions is no.

From the outset, this person is 'just asking' you to do all the work. That's why in just two words they have told you everything you need to know about what it would be like to date them.

A
Tinder Translator

TL;DR

Someone who has not made the effort to write more than 'just ask' in their bio is not even worth the effort of a right swipe.

B

is for
Banter

"Must have banter."

Translation: Must find my borderline-offensive jokes funny and reflect my own sense of humour back at me. Must not be actually funny in your own right.

Banter. For many modern daters, this one word is an instant turn off. It is, after all, a staple of the douchebag vocabulary.

Was it ever thus? I'm not sure. In the early noughties, I seem to remember it meaning a sort of snappy back and forth. A person who had banter was someone who always had a quip in their back pocket, who could give it out and take it. In my early university days, I definitely prided myself on having banter. But in retrospect, this may have been because I was surrounded by private school boys who, while they didn't fancy me, praised my 'bants' often. And, as a 19-year-old with self-esteem so low I often tripped over it, that was a big deal.

Ah, the male gaze, don't ya just hate it?

I'm pretty sure, though, even if I was just a wide-eyed first year, high off the praise of Posh Boys™, that the meaning of the term 'banter' has deteriorated in the 20 years since. We can't blame dating apps alone for this. Lad culture, perhaps in a backlash to feminist gains, has been increasingly open in its disdain for women who can't take a joke. Of course, those jokes are often belittling and laced with misogyny, but lighten up ladies – it's just banter!

When I read a dating app bio that demands banter, I rarely imagine that the author of said bio will enjoy sharp snapbacks. Quite the opposite: that brand of banter will probably be seen as too serious (I know, the irony). If we point out that these men are full of themselves, or question their motives in a teasing tone, it is not well received. The banter has to be on their terms, and men who can't laugh at themselves rarely like women who do. Or any funny woman, for that matter.

All too often, these men's banter policy is the exact opposite to the one they have on oral sex: they are looking to dish it out but definitely not take it.

B

This leads us to the crux of the matter. The men who ask for 'banter' are rarely asking for someone funny; that's not what they mean. They want someone to laugh at their jokes. And, again, 'jokes' is probably a generous term. They want to be able to make 'edgy' (aka offensive) statements and have you laugh because they're *obviously joking* (more on this in J is for Joking).

And if you don't find their racist or sexist or ableist (the list goes on) views funny? Well, you need to get a bloody sense of humour!

As someone who used to say they loved a bit of banter (the witty back and forth), I find it especially irksome that the word has been so degraded by dudebros. The so-called humour they are keen for you to laugh along with isn't banter at all – it's what I like to call **manter**. But don't tell them that, they will not like it one bit.

---

manter [man • ter] *noun*

Often called 'banter' by its proponents, this form of humour is largely employed by white cishet men and involves being borderline offensive in a way that they feel entitled to be, and then labelling anyone who calls them out as not being able to take a joke.

The thing about men who say they like funny women is that there's a limit to how funny they like their women. Even men who say, and genuinely believe, that they want to date someone who's funny all too often don't really mean it. When they ask for a good sense of humour it is again because they want someone to laugh at their jokes (the less offensive kind). Us making them laugh is a secondary concern, an added bonus. What is important is that they find someone who is savvy enough to really appreciate their hilarity.

It is a rare man who wants someone who is actually *funnier* than he is. I mean, a girlfriend with banter who has the social ease to make your mates laugh occasionally? Excellent. But a woman who is funny enough to hold the room at a dinner party while you laugh along and let her be the centre of attention for a while? That's a harder sell.

No shade to people who want someone who'll laugh at their jokes, by the way. I am one of those people. Sometimes I'll be out at a social event and meet someone who I *just really click with*, you know? Later on, I'll realise that this special connection was mainly based on the fact the other person laughed at all my quips and references, and that was the entire extent of our clicking. Someone finding me funny puts me at ease, I feel accepted and understood. Luckily for me, I am quite funny so it happens a lot.

Still, I once had a man I was in a long-term relationship with tell me that he 'wanted someone he could share his comedy with' when he was breaking up with me. With *me*. Had he met me?

It later transpired that he was sleeping with someone in his comedy improv class who laughed at his shit jokes. Then it all made sense.

If you are a woman who likes to crack a joke, you are sure to have been told by at least one man that you're the funniest girl/woman (let's face it, it's usually girl) he's ever met. They think they are being complimentary saying this, but the subtext has a sting in its tail; you're really funny, *for a girl*. Like, obviously there are loads of funnier men, but well done for reaching the dizzying heights of both having tits and making a man laugh.

B

Tinder Translator

According to *Forbes*, out of the ten highest paid comedians in 2019, only one was a woman (and yes, she was white, cishet and non-disabled).

I genuinely think the whole 'women aren't funny' trope is the patriarchy attempting to manifest a blatant untruth. Women are hilarious.

Next time you're out in a bar, observe tables full of women in comparison with tables full of men. Which groups are absolutely howling with laughter, wiping tears from their eyes while they attempt to compose themselves?

It's not the men, is it?

But if we were to admit that maybe women are as funny as men, even funnier in some cases, we'd have to look at why this myth is perpetuated. Why comedy panel shows still never seem to have a cast where women outnumber men. Why male stand-up comedians out-earn women in almost every case. Why it's so bloody hard to make your voice heard as a woman in a room full of men, unless you conform to what they think is funny.

Even then, you're unlikely to be thought of as both funny *and* attractive.

The funny girl is the one you're mates with, not the hot one you want to fuck. Pick a lane, sweetheart.

Comic actor and utter legend Lily Tomlin said in an interview with *Vulture* in 2013: 'I grew up in a time when women didn't really do comedy. You had to be homely, overweight, an old maid, all that. You had to play a stereotype, because very attractive women were not supposed to be funny – because it's powerful, it's a threat. It takes a long time to change that.'

A lot of women still feel that they have to choose between being funny and being 'feminine'. And, of course, here 'feminine' is code for being attractive to men.

It may seem that I have strayed off the topic of banter here, but I really think it's all part of the same thing. Manter is a dudebro's defence against a world that increasingly holds a mirror up to their mediocrity. These men have carved out a niche (and unfunny) brand of humour for themselves, one that they can gatekeep. One where they still get to say who is and isn't funny. One where they still get to say a lot of things that really aren't, or shouldn't be, acceptable in this day and age.

If we aren't laughing? Well, we just don't have banter.

And if we're the ones making others laugh? Then we are an unusual case of a *quite* funny woman. Or, of course, we are just *a bit too much*.

Ironically, there are very few cishet men who are willing to take the role of straight man in a romantic comedy duo.

As Tomlin says, laughter is powerful, it is life-affirming, it is attention-commanding. And women's roles are all too often framed as giving affirmation and attention to men, not the other way around. I wouldn't say banter is a red flag – an amber one maybe. But what (and who) is and isn't deemed funny by someone can tell you a lot.

B

Tinder Translator

TL;DR

You don't need to spend your time laughing at jokes that aren't funny in order to stroke the ego of a man who, in all probability, won't stroke your clit half as much.

C

is for
Conversation

"Please be able to hold a conversation."

Translation: I don't really want a conversation. I'm not interested in listening to a voice that isn't my own. I am, however, interested in establishing that it is you who must impress/entertain me when we match and not the other way around.

~~~~~~~

The longer you're on dating apps, the more you realise that a lot of it is just dull chat with people you're probably never going to meet. Much like meeting someone at a party, or in a bar, the conversation can flow effortlessly, or it can feel like a robotic exchange of niceties. The latter is the more common situation.

It may shock you to know that I don't lay the blame for this dullness solely at the feet of men (who even am I?). I think maybe we all get a bit battle weary in the game of swipes, or maybe we just aren't as equally excited about all our matches, so we put less effort into some than we do others. Of course, sometimes you're firing off your most charming one-liners and getting nothing back, but I'd be surprised if anyone is offering consistently sparking convo 100% of the time.

Whatever the cause, conversations drier than unbuttered toast abound on the apps. A typical conversation might go something like this:

> Hey
>
> *Hey, Cameron, how's your week going?*
>
> Good yeah, you?
>
> *Pretty good, looking forward to the weekend.*
>
> For sure :)
>
> *What you up to?*
>
> Not much, just working. You?
>
> *Yeah, I'm at work. What do you do?*

Tinder Translator

Blah blah blah.

Of course, for people matching with men, the dullness is all too often spiced up by the introduction of unsolicited (and gross) sexual references. In fact, sometimes the grossness *is* the introduction.

All that is to say that I understand the desire for a decent conversation. It is a longing I can more than empathise with. Wanting a fun, flowing chat with a potential date that doesn't turn smutty within five messages is definitely not a problem. Nor is being irked by the monotony of it all.

Making it a smug and condescending requirement of matching with you, however? That's a dick move, and it sets off alarm bells with me for three reasons.

The first is that it indicates that you think that there are a large number of potential matches that *can't* hold a conversation. You might as well just say 'most of you plebs are too vapid to date an intellectual powerhouse such as myself.' And in a gendered context it definitely suggests that, perhaps, you don't see many women as intellectual equals.

This might sound a bit rich coming from me after I've spent the intro of this chapter outlining my own belief that most dating app chats are dull or gross or a mixture of the two. The difference is that I would never have written in my bio 'please don't be dull or gross'. Because there's no point. Writing stuff like that mostly serves to demonstrate your dissatisfaction; dull and gross dudes will still match you, and now you also look like a prick to the ones who aren't dull and gross.

Secondly, a demand like this sets you up as the person who has to do all the conversational work, and them up as the judge of your conversational skills (see also: A is for Ask). Because they have established, from the outset, that they are great at conversation.

C

Genuine opening lines offered by cis men on dating apps include:

"Can you pee on me?"

"Nice boobs"

"You look like you give a good blow job."

"Are you a washing machine? Because I'd like to fill you up with my dirty load."

"Do you do anal?"

"I just wanked over your photo."

"Can I come over and destroy your pussy?"

And they say romance is dead.

Except, they usually aren't.

Herein lies the most infuriating aspect of this dating app stock phrase – more often than not, people who use it can't hold a fucking conversation!

I asked my Instagram followers if they had ever matched with someone who had 'please be able to hold a conversation' in their bio. Then I asked if that person turned out to be a good conversationalist: 96% said no!

It may not surprise you that entitled men on dating apps can talk the talk but not walk the walk. Well, in this case, they can't even talk the talk, but you get what I mean.

When you really think about that language of *holding* a conversation, it's pretty revealing. *Having* a conversation is a two-way thing; *holding* one implies taking the weight of it. Could it be that folks who make this demand do so because they are not good at holding conversations themselves? Have they added this demand to their bio because more than a few exchanges with matches fizzled out after the initial greetings/basic questions? And could they perhaps be blaming said fizzling out on the wrong party?

There's a common denominator here, Clive, and it's not the women you're chatting with.

One of the key components in a good conversation is asking questions and, crucially, being interested in the answers.

Allow me to demonstrate. We'll start with the asking-questions-for-the-sake-of-it style.

C

> What do you do for work?
>
> *Oh, I'm a teacher.*
>
> Cool.

And here's the asking-questions-because-you-actually-want-to-learn-more-about-the-human-being-you're-chatting-with style:

> What do you do for work?
>
> *Oh, I'm a teacher.*
>
> Ah nice. What's your teacher vibe? Robin Williams in Dead Poets Society or Jack Black in School of Rock?
>
> *Beginning of the film Jack Black, or end of the film Jack Black?*
>
> You tell me.
>
> *Ha! Well I have taught a few lessons hungover ...*
>
> Haha, bet that's fun! What do you teach?

See the difference? Of course you do; you're not a prick.

The problem with many of the people on dating apps who bemoan the lack of good conversation is that they often aren't interested in their matches as fully-rounded humans. Or they think that good conversation should just 'flow', without realising that they may in fact have to make a bit of effort in order to make that happen. But they don't want to make the effort – they want you to do it for them.

Come to me, O women of Tinder, and carry a conversation all the way to my bedroom, where I shall underwhelm you sexually for 5 to 10 minutes!

The third reason I'm wary of the conversation demanders is that what many of these men want is not a conversation at all; they want an audience for their monologues. They know on some level that good listening is a key component of conversation; they just want you to listen to them.

Much like the requirement of having a 'sense of humour' so you can laugh at some douchebag's jokes, being able to 'hold a conversation' all too often means being able listen, enraptured, to some douchebag's mediocre stories of **travelling** in Thailand.

A note on travelling

Travel is not a personality. Beware those who list the number of countries they've been to as if the world exists merely for them to collect experiences. Lots of people have travelled extensively, some haven't travelled at all. It is not an indicator of how interesting or worldly they are. Anyone who has been in a far-flung bar and heard someone shouting slowly 'I WAAANT A BEEEEER' at a barman who probably speaks better English than they do should know this. Of course, you might connect with someone over a shared love of exploring new places, or of a specific country, but this whole '45 countries and counting' bullshit has big coloniser energy.

You don't have to have been on dating apps for all this to sound familiar. If you've talked to more than four men in your life then you have probably been talked over. It doesn't even necessarily have to be about themselves. There are many men who will wax lyrical on any subject, regardless of whether they know anything about it. The word 'mansplaining' is ubiquitous for a reason.

On Instagram I once asked women for examples of cis men chatting shit with a confidence not justified by their level of expertise. I was inundated with responses. Multiple women have told me that they have had their PhD thesis explained to them by less qualified men. Quite a few have had cis men explain the female orgasm to them – right after sex during which the woman did not orgasm.

My personal favourite was the story of the woman who went on a date with a man who proceeded to *explain* to her that mansplaining wasn't a thing and that women were just dramatic (see the next chapter for more on the subject of drama).

Men often have ways of taking up space in conversations without realising it half the time. Having the confidence to speak

Tinder Translator

up is something that is socialised into them, especially if they are also white and/or come from a socioeconomically privileged background. Trust me, I've dated many a Posh Boy™ and the force of misplaced confidence is especially strong in them.

Of course, there are many ways identities can intersect to compound this dynamic. Black women get characterised (often by defensive white women) as aggressive for simply speaking assertively or passionately, while the very same behaviour in white men is praised and romanticised. Disabled people are all too often talked over or infantilised. Trans and non-binary folks are, sometimes deliberately, misgendered and dead-named, the effect of which is to dehumanise and silence them. The world has many ways to quieten those who are not white, cis, male, heterosexual, affluent, middle class and non-disabled.

Taking an interest in others, empathising with them, seeing difference and enquiring about it, is a skill those who experience inequality and marginalisation have to practise. It is basic survival.

Women, for example, must learn how to navigate male environments in a way that is inoffensive. We are taught to massage men's egos – to just 'let it go because he's harmless really' – from a young age. We are taught to adapt our behaviour in order to mitigate a harm that is usually out of our control. Men, especially when they are privileged in other ways, are much less likely to be socialised like this.

And then we add in the fact that basic interpersonal skills such as listening, taking an interest in others and offering compliments or praise are all characterised as feminine traits? And God forbid a man be seen to 'act like a girl'! Bloody hell, they never stood a chance, did they?

That is not to excuse those men who have made it to now and still not cracked the whole two-way conversation thing.

We can understand the forces that mould men into misogynists without concluding that they just can't help it. Because they can.

We all know this because we've all met men who aren't self-centred – who are interested and interesting. Okay, they may seem a rarity in the world of online dating, but we know they're there. In the meantime, the mono-syllabists and monologuers alike are unlikely to make adequate partners for anyone who requires to be seen as a whole actual person. And we should all require that, at the very fucking least.

C

TL;DR

I can hold a conversation but I'm not prepared to carry one, Carl.

D

is for
Drama

"NO DRAMA."

Translation: Don't have emotions or opinions, or challenge me in any way. A personality is acceptable, as long as you tone it down a bit.

If you want to see what a person with no sense of irony looks like, scroll through a dating app until you find someone who thinks the best way to indicate that they want a stress-free relationship is to write a two-word sentence IN ALL CAPS. All caps! The most dramatic of all punctuation choices.

Caps or not, though, 'no drama' is a big red flag, an instant swipe left.

All of us can be dramatic at times, we can all overreact. Ask any parent about the human capacity to tantrum; it is universal. Yet the language of drama is deeply gendered: women are dramatic and emotional. Men aren't. Ignore the thousands of crying, angry, jubilant men in sports stadia the world over – they're not dramatic, just passionate. A group of women behaving in the same way would likely be characterised as a case of mass hysteria.

The very word 'hysterical' has its roots in 19th-century pseudo-science that declared that women displaying signs of distress, anger or depression were suffering from a condition where their silly lady-womb was wandering around their body. (Seriously, that is what hysteria meant, I'm not being dramatic.) Incidentally these were women who also couldn't vote or own property and who could be beaten and raped by their husbands with legal immunity. Can't think why their mental health was taking a hit – a wandering uterus is the only logical explanation.

We have come a long way since those doctors labelled troublesome women as suffering from hysteria, but the 'no drama' crew bears some striking resemblances. (NB: I've since learned that some of those doctors did actually try to treat hysteria with vibrators to make women orgasm, so perhaps they don't have as much in common with the modern day fuckboy as I first thought.)

The urge to label women as insane when they are dissatisfied with the limits of the patriarchy, or upset about just about anything, is definitely a common denominator in all this.

I would bet my house on the fact that what 'no drama' actually means to most of these dudes is, just be a pushover. Be submissive. Smile and nod and give me blow jobs.

D

Tinder Translator

Just don't require any level of commitment or empathy beyond the bare minimum. Most are even ambivalent about the bare minimum, tbh.

What these men count as drama is, for the most part, the natural progression of a relationship, which makes falling for them more dangerous. Because, at first, it won't even be a problem.

It's just emotionally sensible not to dive in headfirst to an all-consuming love affair with a perfect stranger. Protecting yourself – keeping some of yourself back while you get to know each other, assess compatibility, and establish trust – is healthy. In fact, not doing those things can be a red flag in itself.

But as you begin to open up and invest more of yourself, let your feelings deepen a little, that is when you also begin to require a bit more from your partner. And that's when the NO DRAMA men go on the defensive.

Have you ever, after three or four months, tentatively asked if maybe the situationship you've found yourselves in is, you know, going anywhere? Could he, perhaps, see you himself committing to you at some point? How about some basic emotional support from the person you're sharing a bed with multiple times a week? When you tell him you like him (just *like* him), could he return the compliment now and then?

All too often these perfectly reasonable requests are framed as too much. 'Babe, I thought you were chill,' 'I like what we've got, why do you have to get heavy?' or worse, 'Why are you being so sensitive, you know I like you.' Do I though, Derek? Do I?

Any needs at all (we all have them, us humans) will be framed as needy by the men who insist they don't want drama. But God forbid you express feelings of hurt or anger at being characterised as irrational for wanting more than shallow text exchanges, drinks and sex. *There's no need to act like a psycho, babe.*

D

Aileen Barratt

Of course, the assertion from the outset that they're 'not into drama' is a move intent on making sure he never has to meet your needs or engage with your emotions; in other words, he never has to do any actual work in the relationship.

The men who characterise perfectly normal behaviour and needs as dramatic – and by implication ugly and unattractive – often manipulate women into repressing those parts of themselves entirely.

Because you want to keep him interested, not put him off, and he told you from the outset he doesn't like drama. But if what puts him off you is, you know, your whole personality, then, just maybe, he ain't the one.

The problem is that being attractive, being desirable, having the approval of the male gaze rest upon us is so tied up with our self-esteem that we find it hard to really believe that we'd be okay without the approval of men who don't see us as fully human.

We strive to be what Gillian Flynn describes so brilliantly, through the voice of her character Amy in *Gone Girl*, as the 'Cool Girl'. This is the girl who will bend over backwards to please a man, who will laugh at the jokes, listen to the monologues, ask all the questions and feign interest in the answers. The girl who will contort herself into whatever shape it is that her lover finds most pleasing and never asks for anything in return.

After one break-up, long before the time of dating apps, I remember feeling a huge regret at having asked my boyfriend to come and see me when he had said he would. If I'd just let him snort coke with his friends that night, instead of being a buzzkill

D

Tinder Translator

and demanding that he keep the plans we'd made, maybe he wouldn't have dumped me. At no point did I think, 'why would I want to be with someone who dumps me for asking for the bare minimum?'

In that relationship, as in many others that happened when I was much older, I had been the cool, chill version of myself for as long as I could possibly muster. I had accepted the aloof offerings of men who definitely liked fucking me (and who can blame them?), and also seemed to quite enjoy my company, for a month or four, or more. I had tried, as much as possible, to make little to no requirements of them. To rein in my opinions, often my intellect and *always* my feelings.

But guess what? I have feelings. I am a person who feels things very deeply. This can be messy and wonderful and sometimes a combination of the two. And loving me has to include accepting those feelings, that mess. And that's not dramatic or too much for anyone who is worth me loving. The same goes for you.

The NO DRAMA guys will have you believe that it is *you* who is immature or irrational for wanting more than Netflix and poundy sex. Nothing could be further from the truth. It's they who lack the emotional literacy to engage with you. Even if they don't return the feelings you have for them (which is quite clearly ludicrous, as you're an absolute babe) it is easier to dismiss you as dramatic than to have any kind of adult conversation.

And look, it's not all their fault. It's the motherfuckinpatriarchy, of course. In a world where too many men have only been able to cry publicly when their team gets knocked out of a tournament and where the only socially acceptable emotion they can display at any other time is anger, what would we expect?

D

Aileen Barratt

If they admit women expressing emotions isn't, in fact, a flaw, they'd have to ask themselves why they can't do the same. And then things really would start to unravel.

Still, you're not a rehabilitation centre for emotionally stunted men, you are a human being with feelings. You deserve someone who accepts you as such. Frankly, anything else just sounds like too much drama.

TL;DR

Honestly just swipe left on 'NO DRAMA', unless you enjoy being told you're dramatic for having normal human emotions and/or requiring respect.

E

is for
Entrepreneur

"Entrepreneur."

Translation: I might run my own successful business, but it's more likely that I just talk a lot about 'the hustle' and have an over-inflated sense of my own importance.

There are a lot of entrepreneurs on dating apps. A suspicious amount. If there were really that many thriving entrepreneurs around, surely there'd never be an economic downturn again?

In reality the term 'entrepreneur' is vague enough to cover a number of situations: everything from Jeff Bezos to an unemployed man in his mum's basement with an idea for an app (I'd rather date the app guy than Jeff tbh – big Lex Luthor energy).

I am sure that some of the people who use the title 'entrepreneur' do so to hide their embarrassment at being unemployed, and I have no desire to mock that. There are a whole host of reasons that someone might not have a paid job – from disability to lack of access to childcare – and our society has wrongly normalised shaming people in these situations. Under the patriarchy, this can weigh especially heavily on men, who are socialised as the 'providers' and to believe their work and wealth is a measure of their worth.

If someone is concealing their circumstances, though, that's a bad sign. It speaks to not being okay with where they are at – and possibly being in denial about it. However much you might empathise with someone feeling like that, I do not recommend starting a relationship with them. Still, they aren't who I want to talk about here.

Neither do I want to talk about the ones who call themselves entrepreneurs as a code for the fact they trade in illegal substances. I'm all for the decriminalisation of drug use, but I hope I don't have to explain to you the inherent dangers of dating a drug dealer.

I want to talk about the flashy types (who are also sometimes drug dealers, to be fair). The ones who use the word 'entrepreneur' – or 'CEO' or 'company director' – when 'self-employed' or 'small business owner' might do because they want to impress you as much as they impress themselves, a feat that is likely impossible to achieve. They may even have a regular day job that they don't feel suits their BDE (Big Dicked Entrepreneur) facade.

E

You're not an entrepreneur, Eric, you're an estate agent who dabbles in crypto-currency.

I'm happy to mock these shiny-suited, ego-driven dudebros. These guys are to be spotted on the apps posing by sports cars they don't own or with bottles of Grey Goose on ice in the club. Be still my beating labia. Dates with them are all too often like listening to a sales pitch that you never asked for, for a product you don't want. Dull as fuck.

I often think that peacocking about money or posing by flashy cars is to men what using beauty filters is to women. All the mean stuff men will say about women whose photos are all obviously heavily edited – that they are shallow or fake, for example – is exactly what we think when we see the carefully curated pics of them living their 'best life'.

Ironically, it's all too often these same guys who write 'no duck pouts or Snapchat filters' in their bios. Because, sure, Ethan, it's just us girls who are shallow.

Declaring yourself an entrepreneur is, in many ways, the verbal equivalent of being photographed standing next to a Maserati in white chinos. It could be an accurate representation of your lifestyle, but 99% of the time it's just bullshit.

I'm reliably informed by my straight male sources that women rarely use this term on the apps. Quelle surprise. In fact, many women who are financially successful often underplay this aspect of their life.

One friend of mine, who worked in property before starting her own business, says men are often intimidated when they find out that she owns two properties. Ironically, these same men seem less threatened by her (very successful) small business,

Telle Moi, perhaps because it primarily caters to women. *Oh, you sell nail polishes? Cute.*

The idea of a woman earning more or being more successful than her male partner is still seen as unusual and potentially problematic. Women know this, and it can lead many of us to instinctively play down our achievements in order not to put men off. This is despite the fact that any man put off by your achievements is not one whose interest is worth having.

There are plenty of articles advising both men and women on how to deal with the *ker-razy* circumstance of finding yourself in a relationship where the woman earns more than the man. Headlines, often based on academic studies, proclaim 'men get stressed when their wives make more money than they do' or even 'this one thing in your marriage increases the risk of divorce by 33%'. Then there are the countless forum threads on whether men would date women who earned significantly more than them, or women would date men who earned less than them.

This relationship pressure is not caused by the money itself, of course. No one is conducting studies into how women who earn less than their male partners feel about it. Cos that's just, like, normal, isn't it? Thanks, gender pay gap! No, it's only when women earn more than men, or indeed outstrip them in any other way (that doesn't involve caregiving), that issues arise.

It's almost as if we live in a sexist world that teaches boys and men that being with a successful, powerful or independent woman is emasculating in some way.

Here's what I think you should do if a man who seems otherwise lovely calls himself an entrepreneur. Ask a few questions – partly because you're interested and partly to detect potential bullshit. If you ask them what they actually do and they only offer something

vague about Bitcoin or NFTs or just having big plans, then it's safe to say that they don't have a lot going on, but they think a lot of themselves.

Not that jobs are a great indicator of being a grown-up. Someone can have everything sorted on the surface and still be a child underneath.

The only thing that will tell you if a man is on your level of maturity is the way he behaves towards you, not whether he plays the stock market or owns a penthouse apartment.

So, there's a little tip from Aunty Aileen.

I once dated a 40-year-old man with a house, a business and a 12-year-old child he co-parented. *Yes,* I thought, *an actual adult! He won't be a sketchy commitment-phobe.*

Oh, silly, naïve girl.

We went on two dates, but we were busy people and it seemed tricky to find times we were both free. I had a couple of hours one afternoon and I asked if he was free. He invited me to his house, but not for lunch or anything nice and grown-up. He said that the living room was a mess due to his lodger (long story) but we could hang out in his bedroom and watch Netflix. Pretty sure he added some sort of winky face emoji too.

I declined. His invitation basically amounted to: 'use your minimal free time to turn up at my door and have sex with me!' Hard pass.

After that, the guy became pretty sketchy and we didn't see each other again.

I think that's when I finally realised that circumstance isn't a great indicator of being a grown-up. Someone can have everything sorted on the surface and still have nothing of substance to offer.

And that's the problem with the entrepreneur/CEO types of Tinder. By and large they think it's their outward achievements, their conspicuous wealth, that matters.

And, you know, I get it. Fuck, it *is* what matters to a lot of people, in a lot of places. But if you scratch the surface and find there's not much underneath aside from an inflated ego, I'd move on to someone else. The free Grey Goose just isn't worth it.

TL;DR

If being an entrepreneur is his whole personality, maybe he doesn't have a personality?

F

is for
Fun

"Looking for some fun."

Translation: Sex, I am looking for some sex.

'Fun' was the first euphemism I noticed on Tinder.
It's used so ubiquitously to indicate that a person
wants casual sex that that seems to have become
its only meaning. So, be warned, if you agree to
meet up with someone for some fun, they will
not be planning an elaborate date involving
fairground rides and candy floss. More's the pity.

I have had many dating app chats with men who ask 'so, what are you looking for on here?' after about five messages. This almost always means that they are trying to establish whether you want to date in the hopes of forming some sort of relationship (super intense tbh) or are open to a more non-committal casual sex situation.

When this question is mirrored back at them, the answer is almost always the same: 'I'm just looking to have some fun.' That'll be the non-committal casual sex situation, then.

Because I'm me, I have directly asked several blokes what kind of fun – the sex kind or other kinds? They'll inevitably say both, even though they could probably take or leave any other kinds if they were honest.

And look, don't get me wrong. Sex is fun! Or at least it can and should be. There is nothing wrong with people of any gender going on dating apps looking for a safe, casual hook up. The only irksome thing about this particular euphemism is that casual sex often isn't that fun if you're a cis woman hooking up with a cis man. It really depends on whether your prospective partner in the endeavour is interested in making the fun a mutual thing.

Because here's a little fact you may not know: women like sex.

A lot of us really, really like sex. Contrary to popular opinion, we don't necessarily need an emotional connection for it to feel good. We just need to do it with someone who understands consent, cares about our pleasure and knows the basics of our anatomy. Granted, that combination is rarer than it should be when your partners of choice are cishet men.

Of course, there's no foolproof way to gauge whether a new person will be a good sexual partner. But if the only times they are willing to talk about sex directly is during explicit sexting or with cagey vagaries about 'fun', the signs aren't looking promising.

F

It's not just dating apps where people lack the ability to have an adult conversation about sex, although men clearly feel comfortable being more sexually explicit online than they would in person.

The lack of inhibition could actually be a really healthy thing, and make for better sex all round. It could mean that potential matches engage in frank communication about what kind of sex they like, or what their boundaries are. But, certainly when it comes to heterosexual pairings, this is just not the case; see the list of gross opening lines in C is for Conversation for just a few examples of how men on dating apps talk about sex.

It is actually wild how many men are out there cock-blocking themselves on dating apps.

I can't count the number of times that men who I might have slept with have ruined their own chances by crossing lines without first establishing if I was comfortable with them being crossed. Turning straight from suggestive flirtation to some deeply unappealing declaration such as 'I can't wait to bend you over' will kill the mood for me in an instant. And I know I'm not alone.

And it's always that, isn't it? Men who abruptly turn the conversation to sex rarely talk about gently playing with your nipples or running their fingers seductively up your thighs. It's straight to some sort of Pornhub-inspired speed-thrusting scenario. How do you know I want to be bent over, Felix? How do you know I want to be fucked hard? Have you even thought about what I want?

Reader, he has not.

A friend of mine, Kate, who runs the excellent Instagram page @ThirtySomethingSingle, conducted a little social experiment

F

on dating apps back in 2020. She asked men who were either potential hook-ups or who had already made sexual advances one question: 'What's your favourite way to make a woman cum?'

The answers she received were as depressing as they were hilarious. One guy seemed to think that looking a woman in the eye while thrusting hard was enough to do the trick. Are your eyes magical, sir? Needless to say, in all of the answers there were lots of references to pounding and very few to the clitoris. Sigh.

Incidentally, I think the best response to this question would be 'it depends what she likes, I like to make a woman cum the way that's best for her, communication is key'. THAT'S HOT. But 'with my finger/tongue on her clit' would also be more than acceptable.

I have no doubt that the same men who think they can make any woman cum with a good pounding are the ones who will tell their prospective partners they are just looking for some fun. Because it's not your fun they're concerned with; it's theirs.

Studies show that around 80% of people with vaginas can't orgasm from penetration alone.

This lack of concern can often also express itself in a reticence around wearing condoms. Anyone who's had more than one sexual encounter with a cis man has probably been hit with the 'it feels so much better without it' line. Oh really? Well it feels much better to me when I'm not worrying about pregnancy or STIs and I feel like I'm having sex with someone who respects my boundaries, so I guess we're at an impasse.

I was once dating a guy who had been in a two-year relationship previously. He was telling me how his ex-girlfriend had been on

F

Tinder Translator

the pill for the first year but she'd had some side effects so they switched to using condoms. He finished this story by saying, 'See, aren't I good?' Yep, he thought that wearing condoms so his girlfriend didn't have adverse reactions to hormonal pills was somehow a sacrifice and proved that he was a great boyfriend. The bar is low. And I'm ashamed to say that I nodded along at the time. I should have got up and left right there and then.

I distrust any man who blurts out the phrase 'I don't like condoms'. Because no one *likes* condoms. For the most part, if you ask people what their favourite bit of sex is, they won't say fumbling around to find a Durex.

So what do men expect when they say this to women they're sleeping with? I think it's one of two things. The first is that they're hoping to manipulate you into saying you're fine with them not wearing one (there's that Cool Girl thing again). The second is that they want some sort of medal for the very basic act of using contraception. You don't get a cookie for using condoms, my dude. Have you ever heard a woman fish for compliments for going on the pill? You know, the kind of contraception that has actual side effects? No, because we're not entitled pricks who think our access to sex and pleasure should come with no barrier – literally.

Too many men seeking casual encounters see the women they date (and date is a generous term) as an entertainment source at best and a fleshlight with boobs at worst. So, while we can't blame ourselves for the odd disappointing sexual encounter, I'd always proceed with a healthy dose of cynicism when offered a night of 'fun' by a cishet man.

TL;DR

Casual sex isn't 'fun' when you skip the foreplay, Franklin.

G

is for
Good Vibes

"Good vibes only."

Translation: I hide my inability to deal with conflict or, indeed, the full spectrum of human emotion behind a façade of being a really positive person who just, like, can't be around negativity.

The phrase 'good vibes only' (also known as 'positive vibes only') is always popping up on dating apps. Perhaps you even have it in your bio. So before I go in on a certain brand of good-vibers let me make it clear that this phrase alone is not, in my opinion, a red flag. Lots of people who write it just mean 'keep it light' or 'don't be a dick'. Both of these wishes are fair, especially given the hellscape any woman dating men will face on dating apps. But, just so you know, if you put this in your profile, you're keeping company with some absolute experts in passive aggression.

The good vibes lot share many characteristics with the NO DRAMA types. Except these guys go further. They took the advanced class. They would never tell you that you were being too dramatic; that's way too direct. Instead, they'll suggest that maybe you need to meditate more because you seem pretty uptight? Or tell you it's just really hard to be around you when you're like this, because they just find negativity really draining, you know?

And what is being 'like this'? Anything that isn't their definition of good vibes.

Maybe you're tired, maybe you're down, maybe you're unhappy with their behaviour. Whatever it is, it's really harshing their buzz.

Many good-vibers often also describe themselves as spiritual. I say *describe themselves* very deliberately here. I don't mean people who have an actual, non-performative spiritual practice that helps to ground them and connect them with their fellow human beings. In my experience, genuinely spiritual people are humble and have a deep concern for others.

I mean those who see being 'spiritual' as a personality trait, one that makes them superior to the more mundane among us. The men who wax lyrical about kundalini and toxic energy, or the white dudes sporting culturally appropriated, dubiously washed dreadlocks who tell their girlfriends they just aren't on the same level because they haven't done enough acid (yes, that's a thing).

These spiritual good-vibers always have advice or, as I like to call it, **jizzdom**, to offer. You should try transcendental meditation. You should take more magic mushrooms. You should do this sex thing that would be really 'freeing' for you, and just happens to

be something they like and want to do. They might tell you that your base chakra is blocked and they know how they could help you out with that. (If you just threw up in your mouth reading that, my deepest apologies, but please know that I also did while writing this. Solidarity.)

---

jizzdom *[jizz • dom] noun*

Platitudes and/or advice delivered with misplaced confidence in the language of emotional intelligence so that it sounds like wisdom but is, on closer inspection, utter wank.

Apart from the sex stuff, which is coercive bullshit, these suggestions could be well-meaning, if pretty fucking annoying. Except in the context of dating and relationships, the subtext is often 'be more like the person I want you to be'. Or even 'be less yourself'. And, in the end, that shit hurts.

If the man you're with wants you to be some sort of transcendent goddess, then coming home to you on the sofa watching *Love Island* is really gonna disappoint him.

I spent a long time in a relationship with a 'spiritual' man who I felt I disappointed. He was very good vibey. He didn't like going to restaurants (which I love doing) because kitchens were chaotic and angry places and the bad vibes got into the food. Yep. Even when I would cook for us at home, if I listened to aggressive hip-hop or grime (my absolute faves), he'd come in and sing yoga chants over the food to dispel the aforementioned aggressive vibes. That made me feel awful, but he was so *good* so

I just stopped listening to my music when I cooked. In the time we were together, I slowly filed down my own edges so as not to spike his positive vibes. Spoiler alert: turns out I wasn't the disappointing person in that relationship.

And mine isn't the only experience of good-viber nonsense; I've had the displeasure of hearing many a tale from my Instagram community. Some are hilarious, some are infuriating, many are both.

One man said he was always going to be late because he *transcended time*. He said that with a straight face. Another wouldn't shower because it *reset his energy*. Don't think about it too much. A guy answered the Bumble prompt 'I feel most empowered when …' with 'I'm practising squats in the mirror naked with a boner. It's a spiritual thing, you wouldn't get it.' Was he joking? Maybe. But I think we've all encountered men who'd probably regard their own erection as 'a spiritual thing'.

You'll also find members of the 'I don't like condoms' brigade in the good vibes crew (they are a diverse group). One guy told a follower of mine that he didn't wear protection because it would mean they 'couldn't share energy'. If by 'energy' you mean a child and/or venereal diseases, sir, then yes.

One joker's response to having cheated on his girlfriend and given her an STI was to say, 'I can't help it if I have too much positive energy to give!' The audacity is strong in this one.

And that's the thing, these douchebags will demand good vibes about *everything*. Including their own fuckery. They want everything to be nice and good all the time, even when they've been horrible and bad.

G

Tinder Translator

'Look babe, I just can't deal with this negative energy, I'm a free spirit!' Well, Graham, consider your spirit freed because we are not in the business of entertaining this level of nonsense. Nope. No way. And yes, that was very negative, which is appropriate under the circumstances.

Look, constant negativity is not the one, obviously. If the food is crap every time you're out to dinner, and they never have a good word to say about your friends; if every film you watch together is rubbish or they're always comparing you unfavourably to other women? That is some shittily negative energy, get rid. But, similarly, someone who doesn't allow any negativity at all is a massive red flag. It's a sign that they are not able to deal with normal human shit. Because no one is only positive; that isn't a thing.

You are allowed to be sad and angry and messy and moany. Within reason, of course, but all of those things are totally normal.

At the beginning of relationships we all repress our more negative traits. As someone who lives with depression and anxiety, I defo don't lead with that information. But after a while, if the person I'm with can't handle that sometimes I get down, what's the point in being with them? So I can have fun pretending to be Little Miss Sunshine? No thanks, I'd rather wait for someone grown-up enough to know that demanding perpetual positivity is, in fact, the bad vibe

G

TL;DR

I require only good vibes from the toys in the bottom drawer of my bedside cabinet. Actual humans have range.

H

is for
Height

"6'2", because apparently that matters."

Translation: I am well aware that it matters. I have been coasting through the dating world on my height alone since I had a growth spurt aged 17. It's still the most attractive thing about me.

Do you have a preference for dating tall men? You're not alone. Just watch any dating show where women are asked what their type is and wait for pretty much every one of them to include 'tall' in their list of requirements. Men know this too, of course. Men of all heights, which must kind of suck for the shorter ones.

Whenever I post a bio on my grid where the height is listed as 6' – no matter what other awful shit this man might be saying – there's always at least five comments that go something like 'I bet he's 5'9". So what, Hannah? He's just said 'no fat chicks' but you're concerned that he might be … the average height for a man? Cool.

I know that's not necessarily what the commenters are getting at. They are saying that men often lie about their height on dating apps, and that lying on your bio is not a good omen. I agree.

But the way a lot of women (and men) talk about short men, I can't entirely blame them for exaggerating – or omitting – this information. It comes from the same kind of insecurity that makes people who've gained weight upload photos from their thinner days, or balding men wear hats in every picture. Is it deceptive? I guess. But do I get it? Totally.

The world has a very narrow definition of what attractive is, and many of us spend a lot of our dating days trying to stuff ourselves into that restrictive box.

Before I sound all holier than thou, I should make it clear that I have not been immune to this penchant for a taller man. There's been many a time that I was on the fence about matching with a guy on an app and then saw his height listed as over 6' and decided to swipe right. Shallow much?

In Australia, the UK and the USA the average height for a man is 5'9", with only around 15% of men being 6' and over.

H
Tinder Translator

'Hang on!' I hear you cry. 'It's okay to have a physical preference and date accordingly, isn't it?'

Well yes, sort of. Maybe. And I suppose it depends on the purpose of your swiping. If you're looking for a straight-up physical attraction accompanied by hot sex (which is legit) then it's less limiting. If you're looking for someone whose personality you actually like, I'd argue that pushing the boundaries of what you find attractive, or at least questioning the origin of those preferences, might be worth a shot.

Because people say they have a preference for all kinds of things, but often these preferences are bound up in prejudice and/or fetishisation.

Rejection of or attraction to people on the basis of their race, weight, height, disability, gender identity and more can all be explained away as just preferences. And maybe some are, but in a society that constantly screams from every billboard that white, thin or muscular, cis, tall, non-disabled bodies are both the 'norm' and the most attractive, we owe it to ourselves – as well as everyone else – to at least ask some questions.

It won't surprise you to learn, then, that I think most of the preference for tall men is rooted in patriarchal norms, and that we should work at rejecting them in ourselves. Not because you should give the short dudes a chance (although that may happen) but because all too often we are taught that to be an attractive, a good, an acceptable woman, we should be small. Or least smaller than men.

That's right: strap in friends, the misogyny I'm going after in this chapter is internalised.

H

Aileen Barratt

The idea that women should be tiny birdlike creatures, dainty damsels, is drummed into us from a young age. Disney has a lot to answer for in that respect. The princesses are without fail at least six inches shorter than their princes in height, and about a quarter of their width. As a girl who was 5'9" at 14, I never quite fit that image. I felt too big in so many ways. We are taught not to take up space with either our personality or physicality, and I have always done both.

It took me most of my life so far to see that wanting a 6'4" rugby player to pick me up in his big strong arms was due more than anything to the fact that it would make me feel like I was a proper, pretty, feminine girl. I never would have said this aloud, or even consciously thought it – I've always been too feminist for that. But there was, beneath it all, a longing to be small and, therefore, more loveable. Bleurgh.

Of course, that's not the case for everyone. Women who are shorter than average often express a wish to be taller, because their stature means they aren't taken seriously, especially in professional contexts. And I guess that tracks, because if short = feminine, then it might be attractive, but it certainly doesn't belong in the board room.

Many taller women will also say that they don't care about height differences; it's the men they date that tend to. This can express itself in controlling behaviour such as not 'letting' you wear heels. (If a man ever tries to not let you do anything, tell him to jog on!) It can even result in putting you down to make himself feel bigger.

And yes, some short men do behave like that. But it's not because they're short – it's because they are dickheads who take their insecurities out on you. And there are insecure dickheads of all heights, as I am sure you're aware.

Some of the best men I've dated have been shorter than me and they've never given a flying fuck about it. Unfortunately, such was my own self-consciousness about being a big ungainly giant (I know, I know, such is the inner critic!) that I would often still police myself into not wearing heels and such nonsense because I so wanted to be someone that I could not physically be: a Disney princess.

Of course, none of us can be a Disney princess – we'd look disproportionate and ridiculous. But since when were beauty standards ever supposed to be, you know, actually attainable? That would surely defeat the object.

Still, I have felt all this and more.

I've tried in so many ways to shrink myself for men, often succeeding for a while, only for my long limbs and loud thoughts to eventually burst out of their restrictive casing and spoil the illusion.

I have also definitely given some douche canoes more attention than they deserve because they were tall. I have, too many times, added 'and he's tall' to the list of attractive traits when describing a new love interest. As if tall is anything other than a genetic chance, as if it's a personality trait.

So, yes, the lads on dating apps do know it's important, and we can mock them for it if we like, but it'll make a lot of us absolute hypocrites.

If you like a big man partly because he helps you feel a bit less big, then you may be discounting some great men in order to assuage an insecurity that is, essentially, sexist, and likely also

Aileen Barratt

77

fatphobic and **ableist**. We *know*, or at least I hope we all do, that 'men should be big and women should be small' is a ridiculous, outdated, binary statement – so it's time we challenged it in ourselves and others.

A note on ableism and dating

Sexism is not the only factor that influences height stigma and height preference; as with many other physical preferences in dating, scratch the surface and you'll find ableism. This isn't something that I would necessarily be cognisant of on my own, and it's certainly not something I can speak on with any authority, but I have learned a lot from listening to disabled voices. I think the best I can do in this context is point you to some of those voices, rather than try to summarise the complex and exhausting landscape of sex and dating for people with disabilities in any tokenistic way here. It was the writer and influencer @CathyReayWrites who first alerted me to my oversight when talking about height. I have listed other fantastic disabled creatives in the 'go and follow' section at the back of this book. For now, I'll leave you with this question: are your physical preferences excluding disabled folks from being your possible partners?

TL;DR

Maybe you like
tall men, maybe it's
the patriarchy.

I

is for
Inked

"Inked."

Translation: I have tattoos. You can see this in literally all of my pictures. But I am still mentioning them here because they are, in fact, my entire personality.

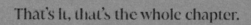

That's it, that's the whole chapter.

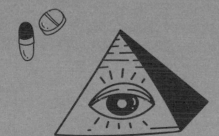

J

is for
Joking

"Chill out, it was just a joke."

Translation: I've tried to push your boundaries and/or generally been gross, but now you're calling me out on it so I'll pretend I was never serious in the first place.

Have you heard of the phenomenon called 'Schrodinger's douchebag'? (I have tried to find the source of this term to no avail, but the person who coined it is a genius.) A Schrodinger's douchebag is someone who makes an unacceptable remark and decides on whether they were serious or joking based on the reaction they get.

Here's an example of how 'it was just a joke' might play out on a dating app:

> So, what you doing tonight?
>
> *Just having a quiet one,*
> *probably watch some TV.*
>
> Ah yeah? How about I
> come round? We could
> watch some porn ... or
> make some of our own.
>
> *Um no. That's really*
> *inappropriate. I would never*
> *invite a man I didn't know*
> *back to my house anyway.*
>
> Alright, chill out, I was only
> joking. You need to relax.

Sound familiar? It is to me too.

The thing is, these guys aren't joking, not really. They are testing the waters, seeing what they can get away with. If a woman replied to these over-zealous advances with 'omg, yes I would love that, come straight on over!' I doubt very much that Jason would stick to the it-was-just-a-joke script.

Hiding behind alleged humour doesn't just apply to unwanted sexual advances either. Declaring they were only joking is a classic way for those who make prejudiced remarks to avoid accountability.

It should be no surprise, then, that the 'it was a joke' defence is actually a well-documented rhetorical device of the far right. In her horrifying and essential book, *Men Who Hate Women*, Laura Bates documents the workings and ideologies of the so-called manosphere: a network of extremist misogynists (such as incels and men's rights activists) whose views trickle down into mainstream thinking. These groups have strong links and overlaps with the alt right, as Bates makes clear.

One of the tactics of the far right is to employ a tone that they can always brush off as irony when they are called out. In her book, Bates refers to a 'style guide' written by neo-Nazi Andrew Anglin for his extremist website, which will remain nameless. The so-called style guide was acquired and published in full by *The Huffington Post* in 2017 and is a chilling insight into the self-aware, calculated recruitment tactics of the alt-right.

The whole text is laden with vile racism, sexism and misogyny, as well as rampant, overarching anti-Semitism. Despite this, Anglin continually insists that the tone of the website should be 'light'. Saying things like 'generally, when using racial slurs, it should come off as half-joking' and 'the unindoctrinated should not be able to tell if we're joking or not'.

The ambiguity of humour used by racists and misogynists is a ploy to fish for willing recipients of their ideology.

Meanwhile, they can dismiss those who criticise them as not being able to take a joke. That's right, the creeps on Tinder and the trolls of the dark web are sometimes singing from the same hymn sheet.

Often (but not always) unaware of their Nazi bedfellows, cishet men online use these same tactics to be super inappropriate with women. And when I say be super inappropriate, I pretty much mean sexual harassment, but this particular form of douchebaggery has become so commonplace we rarely think of it like that anymore.

Being pestered for nudes or graphically propositioned by someone you've barely exchanged pleasantries with is something many women have simply resigned themselves to. Just like with street harassment or walking home with our keys between our knuckles, it's part of the price we pay for not being men.

Actually, when I think about it like that, it's a fair exchange. Imagine being a man.

That was sarcasm. Sort of.

There is, undoubtedly, a level of shit that women are expected to put up with because that's just how it is. When we push back against that, we get labelled as prudes or stuck-up or told we need to learn to take a joke.

Jake wasn't *actually* suggesting we get our tits out on Snapchat – he was obviously joking ladies!

It's an accusation often launched at feminists – that we are humourless, flat-chested husks of women, bitter in the face of male rejection and having a strop en masse. I even get it on my Instagram page. It never fails to amuse me when men (it's

Tinder Translator

always men) comment 'jeez, you need to lighten up, it's not that deep' on one of my satirical takes on a dating app bio. Gleefully replying 'it's just a joke dude, chill out' is one of the great joys of my life.

It is a delicious irony that the majority of blokes who go around accusing others of being humourless snowflakes can't actually take a joke, or even a slight dig, when it's aimed in their direction.

Yes, Piers Morgan, I'm looking at you.

Another favourite phrase of these jokers is 'if you're easily offended, we won't get on'. I would bet my house that everyone with this in their bio makes at least one sexist, racist, homophobic, transphobic, Islamophobic, antisemitic or ableist comment a day. So, to be fair to them, they're right, we won't get on.

I used to get riled up by the accusations that I was too uptight. Why couldn't I just let things go? Was I killing the mood? Was I taking it all too seriously? Nah. I love a laugh. I just don't love dickheads who do or say harmful and offensive shit and think they can get away with it by employing the 'it was a joke' loophole.

Beware of the men (or anyone really) who try and silence your criticism in this way. Or who mask their pervy predilections with a joke-disclaimer. They are testing the waters, seeing what they can get away with. It's toddler behaviour – keep pushing the boundaries to see if they give way. But unfortunately for this lot, we're on to them. And we're only dating grown-ups from now on.

J

Aileen Barratt

TL;DR

I'm only into jokes
that make me
laugh, so it's a
hard pass on this
set of jokers.

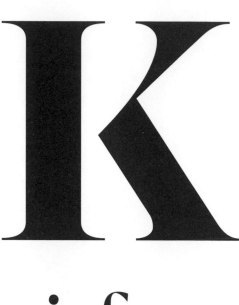

K

is for
Kinky

"Swipe right if you're kinky."

Translation: I wouldn't know the first thing about consensual, playful kink. I just describe myself as a Dom because I like hitting, choking and hair-pulling without asking whether or not my sexual partner will enjoy it.

Sometimes I think about how much better sex would be if every man who mentioned kink in their bio knew the first thing about the world of BDSM. How much more playful, consensual and exciting the landscapes of intimacy and desire would be if they were as enthusiastic about communication, consent and aftercare as they were about spanking and spitting.

Too often, though, men (especially cishet men) who include some reference to BDSM or kink in their dating app bios have one central desire – to be violent and abusive to women during sex.

You only have to pull up the homepage of Pornhub to see that so many acts, from hair-pulling to restricting airways, have become the norm. Unfortunately, what hasn't moved over into the mainstream is the culture of care and communication that is central to the kink community. Instead, we are left with often violent acts of domination – almost always by men to women – being depicted as sexually enjoyable for all parties (porn actresses really can sell it).

A lot of us vaguely know that there are sex parties, clubs and even fetish apps, but most have no idea of the amount of boundaries and self-policing that goes into making those spaces safe and enjoyable. There's a lot that those of us who engage in vanilla sex (and we'll talk about all the ways the term 'vanilla' is incorrectly used to shame and coerce women in V is for Vanilla) could really learn from.

The principles around sharing and practising kink are commonly expressed as either Safe, Sane and Consensual, or RACK (risk-assessed/aware consensual kink). Boundaries are discussed before anything takes place, safe words are shared if needed, and if someone is known to have violated boundaries and agreements then others are warned and that person is no longer welcome in the community.

People who enjoy and engage in BDSM discuss their needs for aftercare before they get down to business. Some people like cuddles, or to discuss how they feel about the scene (the term used for the sexual scenario they have created with each other), or they want to shower straight after, or whatever. Even if you're only meeting for sex, your responsibility to each other doesn't end at the point of orgasm. Aftercare is a big part of the incredibly mature approach to sex that exists within many of these communities.

K

Of course, as I said before, most men who claim to be kinky, and/or to be looking for someone who is, are unaware of any of these concepts.

There is a frightening number of fuckboys who call themselves Doms, or 'dominant' in bed, on dating apps. These men rarely mean they are seeking a playful, consensual, pre-agreed scenario where a woman whose kink is submission engages in mutually satisfying sex. They mean they want to hit you and call you a slut.

And look, if that's what you're into, great! I've had some fun being submissive in sexy situations before, no judgement. But it was mostly fun because I knew the guy I was doing it with was aware that I liked it too. We discussed boundaries, we chatted after sex about what we liked and didn't. It felt mutual and safe.

Too often, though, no conversation takes place. The blame for this lies largely with the dual phenomena of widely available violent porn and books like *Fifty Shades of Grey* – both of which imply that what women really want is to be dominated.

But if even being a billionaire who looks like Jamie Dornan doesn't excuse the emotionless, controlling sexual appetite of Christian Grey (and I'd like to emphatically state that it doesn't) why should we accept that behaviour from Keith the accountant off of Tinder?

Too many women are subjected to acts of domination and degradation without being asked if they want it. And let me be clear: that's not kink, it's abuse.

In what other context could someone hit, insult or strangle you and have you think 'well, I guess that's just what he's into'?

I have spoken to dozens of women who have had scary, and often painful, experiences at the hands of male sexual partners. Being spat at, slapped round the face and called horrible degrading names are not rare events; they are all too common.

Some will say 'he was lucky I shared his kink' when reporting those stories. And while I am super glad they weren't traumatised by the experience, I'm not sure it's helpful. Because, sure, you liked what he did, but *he didn't know you would*. And men who enjoy inflicting pain on women, or degrading them in other ways, without prior knowledge that it's a turn on for them, are walking red flags.

We have to ask ourselves why they would enjoy that. Why do they want to hurt us?

Sure, some assume that 'all girls like it', whatever *it* is, but they are likely to be the same guys who have never actually asked a woman what she likes.

Often during sex with men, women don't feel safe to say stop or express that they aren't enjoying themselves, so the guys go on assuming they are some sort of stud. One woman told me about a man who had done something non-consensual during sex, and when she'd confronted him about it he'd said it was 'easier to apologise than to ask for permission'. So that's, you know, incredibly chilling.

Out of all the non-consensual and scary acts I regularly hear about, choking (or strangulation, as I like to more accurately call it) is by far the biggest theme. Some women report almost every new partner doing something 'chokey' without consent. It's certainly happened to me, and to be honest I didn't used to mind it. It wasn't until a couple of years ago that I began to learn just how dangerous it is. Spoiler alert – it's really fucking dangerous.

K

In a survey of women who sleep with men in my Instagram community, 77% of respondents said they had been subjected to a violent or degrading act that could be misconstrued as BDSM (spanking, hair-pulling, spitting, insults) without giving prior consent. And 60% reported being strangled non-consensually during sex.

If kink is a spectrum, then breathplay (which is what choking and other forms of airway restriction are called in the BDSM community) is right at the 'wow this is really fucking risky' end. A lot of kinksters would not even entertain breathplay as an option, and I have been told by members of the community that some clubs and dungeons have blanket bans on any kind of breath restriction – even if the people who are doing it together have had training and done it a hundred times before. There is always a significant risk of incredibly serious injury or even death with these acts; it makes sense that a safe, risk-aware community may see fit to ban them altogether.

So, on the one hand you have the kink community – who are open to all kinds of shit your average fuckboy would be fully shocked by – saying that choking is super dangerous and should only be attempted by sober, experienced and trained people (and even then maybe not at all) While on the other hand you have drunk dudebros, who aren't even aware that the primary function of breathplay is to heighten your partner's orgasm, throttling women for fun. This seems fine.

Depressingly, these bedroom behaviours are so normalised that many young women don't even think of them as optional. Often they are ashamed to admit they don't really enjoy rough, poundy sex where they are being 'dominated' by men who have made no attempt to arouse them before said pounding. Pounding. Bleurgh.

K

Aileen Barratt

seeing to

given a good

ruined

destroyed

railed

pounded

I often think about how many synonyms
for sex are violent in essence.

smashed

drilled

ploughed

banged

Honestly, the amount of cishet men who think something along the lines of 'I'd destroy that pussy' is a sexy opener is wild. It's like, erm, no thank you sir, I'm actually quite fond of my vagina.

The language we use around sex matters because all of these terms imply a roughness that most people with vaginas will simply not enjoy, unless it's been built up to with lots of other stimulation.

More than this, they are all verbs – they are doing words, they are descriptions of one person doing something *to* another person, rather than *with* them. Heterosexual sex is too often discussed as something men perform and women receive, and I'm sure I don't need to spell out why that's so problematic.

Of course, thinking about sex in this way also limits how men can explore their sexuality. Many young boys watch porn and think they have to play a role that they wouldn't naturally desire. The expectation of aggressive male domination in the bedroom is sad for everyone, but it's especially dangerous for women. You only have to look at the use of the so-called 'rough sex defence' employed by defendants who argue they should have reduced or no culpability because the offence occurred during a 'sex game gone wrong' to see this very clearly.

There is no official data kept by the UK government on this subject, but the campaigning organisation We Can't Consent To This (WCCTT) have found that out of 67 people killed in claimed cases of sex gone wrong, 60 were women and only 7 were men. Even more striking, all suspects accused of causing these deaths were male. At the time of writing, no woman has ever attempted the rough sex defence in a murder trial.

K

Aileen Barratt

Cases such as these have risen significantly over the past decade. In the 1980s and '90s the argument that victims had consented to the acts that injured or killed them were used in UK courts once a year or less. In 2016 that defence was used 20 times, often successfully.

Campaigns from groups like WCCTT mean that the use of the rough sex defence will no longer be admissible in court in the UK, but their work continues to highlight the ways in which violent men will use alleged kink and sex games as an excuse to cause unthinkable harm to their sexual partners.

If you're thinking that this has all gotten a bit heavy, you'd be right. I don't know how to write wry jokes about this stuff. It's just not fucking funny, is it? But it's important. I couldn't write a book about modern dating and misogyny and leave out this horrific and yet ubiquitous aspect.

Most of you reading this are strangers to me (at least I hope you are, or sales will have gone horribly badly), but I care about you. I want you to have fun, pleasurable sex and I really, really don't want you to die. So, if I have to be a buzzkill for half a chapter, so be it!

Pain may excite some people sexually, and it's awesome if you want to play around with that with someone you trust and can talk to. But we *have* to keep challenging the normalisation of men hurting women in heterosexual sex, and the expectation that women should just be okay with it. We have to keep challenging the idea that sex is something men do *to* women – rather than with them. It's fucked up and we all deserve better, more pleasurable and frankly more interesting sex.

TL;DR

He's not kinky, he just likes hurting women.

L

is for
Lone Wolf

"Lone wolf."

Translation: I'll tell you I'm a heartless prick up front so that I can be awful and inconsistent without feeling bad about it.

If you are looking for a relationship, don't match with a man (and it is always men with this one) who calls himself a lone wolf. And if you won't listen to me on the matter, listen to the late, great Maya Angelou: 'When someone shows you who they are, believe them the first time.'

If we all listened to Dr Angelou we would save ourselves a lot of pain. But inevitably we don't. I blame romantic fiction and rom-coms almost entirely for this.

No shade to Jane Austen, *Pride and Prejudice* is a work of art, but if a man is behaving outwardly like Mr Darcy does at the beginning of the book, it is unlikely that he is internally smouldering with love for you or secretly the most honourable person you'll ever meet. That goes for you too, Bridget Jones.

Neither is the sullen, square-jawed boy at school going to soften into a vulnerable, gentle soul who declares their love for you on stage at the prom because he DOESN'T CARE WHAT PEOPLE THINK ANYMORE (see: all teen movies ever).

I could go on, but you get the picture. We shouldn't pin our hopes on any of these fairytales coming true. The lone wolf is not going to turn out to be a vampire who marries you and lives happily ever after with your immortal child and her werewolf boyfriend who used to fancy you. Cripes, when you summarise *Twilight* like that, it's no surprise that a generation of women have warped views of what constitutes romance.

No, the real-life lone wolves are not waiting for the warm embrace of the right woman. Especially not the ones who call *themselves* a lone wolf on *a dating app*.

At worst the guy is going to be an utter prick to you, at best he is warning you outright that he is emotionally unavailable and just wants some, ahem, fun. Either way, listen. He is telling you who he is.

Don't make up a different version of him in your head. It doesn't matter what other indications he has given you of his affections. He might introduce you to his friends. He might kiss your forehead after sex. He might tell you you're the most amazing woman he's ever met. It doesn't matter, he has already told you who he is.

Still need convincing? Fine, I'll tell you a little story.

A few years ago I met a guy on Bumble. Let's call him Logan. Logan was about my age, he had a decent job and he was fun to be around. He was also hot, but wasn't arrogant about it. Looking back, we didn't have much in common, but we laughed together and the sex was great. Without going into great detail, I'll just say that he *really* enjoyed my enjoyment.

About a month into us seeing each other, we were lying in bed after the aforementioned great sex. We were doing that thing you do when you're in the early days, when you tentatively start talking about past relationships. I say 'tentative' because this kind of opening up means, at least in my understanding, that you two might be heading in the relationship direction. Knowing more about the other person's past makes you feel closer to them too. So I was quite enjoying our chat, snuggled up in my bed.

Interrupting the flow of the conversation somewhat, Logan said 'I'm gonna say something about you and me now, if that's okay?'

I said it was okay, as long as it wasn't anything bad. But how could it be? You don't say bad stuff to someone while naked in their bed, right?

Well, Logan proceeded to tell me that he was really enjoying what we had, but he wasn't sure if he wanted a relationship. Cool. Cool cool cool. Not only that, but he went on to say, 'I feel like I've got a heart of stone.' That's right, naked in my bed, this man told me that he thought he was likely to be *incapable of love*.

L

Aileen Barratt

And what did I do? Was I firm with him about my boundaries and protecting my heart? Nope. I told him that was, like, totally fine. I was chill. Because that's what I wanted to be. I wanted to be the Cool Girl that the boys like because I just wasn't needy, you know? Argh.

To be fair to the guy, I think he was genuinely worried about hurting me. Not to the extent that he'd actually call things off. No, he was happy to keep shagging me and enjoying our semi-committed relationship as long as I would let it continue without requiring any emotional depth or, you know, full commitment. But still, he had told me who he was, hadn't he? I just didn't listen.

The day after his heart of stone declaration I told him I didn't mind keeping it casual but that I didn't want to introduce him to my friends if that's how he felt. I think he was mildly taken aback by the stating of a boundary – it was pretty revolutionary for me at that time too. Anyway, we continued dating and having lots of sex. Then a few weeks later he invited me to a gig – a gig that he was going to with his best friends. This was *big*.

Except it wasn't.

There was no subtext in this invitation. Logan was not saying 'hey, I know we said we wouldn't introduce each other to our friends, but I've changed my mind because you are melting my stone heart'. He just wanted to see me that night, probably largely due to the fact that we'd have sex after the gig. And he liked my company. It had no larger significance to him than that. For him, the fact that he'd already told me he wasn't sure about a relationship (and I'll talk about the 'not sure' guys in S is for See What Happens), probably made it less of a big deal, not more.

And this is the point I want to impress upon you. When a man tells you who he is, or what he wants, or that he doesn't know

Tinder Translator

what he wants, listen to that. Lone wolf, heart of stone, whatever. Listen. Because they will likely think that, however else they have behaved towards you, they have already let you know where you stand.

This isn't to say that if you give a lone wolf a chance and become convinced that he's falling for you that it's all your fault. Why wouldn't you think that with someone who tells you're stunning, that you're the funniest girl he's ever met, that the sex you have together is some of the best ever? Why wouldn't you start to believe that the one time he said he was a lone wolf was, perhaps, insignificant? Given all the proof to the contrary, it is perfectly natural that you'd feel this way.

Unfortunately, in this particular context, words speak louder than actions.

I dated Logan for another few months. He broke up with me a couple of days after I introduced him to a group of my friends. So, that was fun.

Yes, it was predictable. If this story wasn't about me, I'm sure I wouldn't have predicted any other outcome. And yet, when I was in it, I decided to hope for a different one. And that wasn't the first time this had happened to me.

These lone wolves can literally tell you you're the kind of girl they could see themselves marrying one day and, as long as they have previously stated they don't want a relationship right now or whatever, still be confused as to how you could have possibly gotten the wrong impression.

L

They might even accuse you of 'causing drama' when you point out the stark inconsistencies.

Some might call that gaslighting, but I'm not even sure it's that deep. I think these dudes genuinely believe they've been upfront with you. And in the most basic way, they have. It can often end up with you feeling silly, like you're the irrational one – not the bloke who said one thing *once* and then thought he could do whatever else he wanted, contradict himself in word and deed with no culpability.

Sure, Liam, that seems fine.

A lone wolf type will have you wondering what's wrong with you, why they don't want you. Their inconsistency can, in the words of Her Majesty Cardi B, have you 'looking in the mirror different'. It's a hard pill to swallow that, however amazing you are, your sweet loving is unlikely to be enough to change the mind of a man who has already decided he doesn't want to commit to you.

What hurts even more is that he might change for someone else. We've all stalked social media profiles only to be shot through the heart by a grid post of them and someone new. *A GRID POST? I never even made his stories.* Don't tie yourself up in knots wondering what she's got that you haven't. Maybe they're better suited, maybe she's happy to play the Cool Girl for longer than you were. Does it matter? Are you gonna change yourself to be more like her for the next guy? No, you are not, because you deserve someone who wants you, not her.

And anyway, did you really wanna be with a man who made you feel like you had to prove your worth as girlfriend material? I fucking hope not, babe.

TL;DR

Wolves can't be tamed, hearts of stone can't be made flesh, but you can tell Logan to fuck off out of your bed.

M

is for
Married

"In a loveless marriage, staying for the kids."

Translation: I haven't paid any kind of quality attention to my wife for the past five years and, frankly, resent that she has less time for me and isn't in the mood for sex since birthing two children and taking on the majority of the domestic load. But, look, I'm an absolute hero for sticking it out regardless. Give me a blow job?

There is an unbelievable number of married men on Tinder. And I'm not talking about the ones who are polyamorous or exploring opening up their relationship. I'm talking about the ones who are secretly on there. Whether for an ego boost, in the hopes of some sexting or in pursuit of an all-out affair, they are legion and they are trash.

The married men (or men in long-term relationships) on dating apps tend to fall into three camps: the ones who are honest about it and present themselves as some sort of erotic novelty; the ones who are honest about it and present themselves as some sort of victim/hero; and the ones who are straight up dishonest. I'll take you through each one.

Let's start out with the most brazen: the guy who will tell you he's 'just being honest' and looking to fill his 'naughty needs' that can't get met at home. He attempts to paint his situation in a sort of sexy, forbidden light. And that might work if he wasn't Martin, a 32-year-old construction worker who is prone to use the **devil emoji** and who wants to do Pornhub sex to (not with) you in the back of his Volvo people carrier. Mind the carseats! 😈

A note on the devil emoji

I know some people use this emoji ironically or for the lols, but in a dating bio? Just stop it. For many women who have waded through the sewage plant that is cishet men's dating profiles, it has major cringe factor. In fact, when I surveyed my followers, 97% said they swipe left whenever they see it. You might as well just write 'I'm a creepy dude' and have done with it.

This first guy is, though, the most honest of the bunch – with himself and everyone else. Because you then have the man who is determined to cast himself as the good guy. You know, the stand-up married man who just wants to secretly have sex with someone who isn't his wife? These men are the kind that will say they are staying for the kids, or that their partners aren't affectionate or that they never have sex anymore. In fact, they

M
Tinder Translator

will often interchange 'loveless' and 'sexless' as if they mean the same thing.

Using the kids as an excuse is nonsense – children don't thrive in unhappy homes, however many parents are there.

The lack of affection/sex excuses may be true to an extent, but these men would rather seek sex elsewhere than reflect on why the mother of their children isn't as up for it as she used to be.

Not to put anyone off, but carrying and birthing a child is traumatic and children are fucking exhausting. Cis men's lives tend to go back to some semblance of normal quite quickly after they become fathers; their careers uninterrupted, their bodies untouched by the whole growing of a human. Not so for women and birthing parents, whose bodies and lives are changed in such a stark way that you can easily lose yourself. The level of unpaid domestic labour you do skyrockets, too.

I think a lot of men just don't get how profound this shift is, and as a result they expect their wives to just be like the girl they met before she pushed people out of her vagina, fed them at all hours, lost her social life, became defined as a mother first and foremost, and had the world judging whether she was doing it right the whole time.

Even without children, moving in together can often see the domestic load – both practical and mental – fall increasingly on women in heterosexual partnerships. And that, coupled with a partner who doesn't notice and isn't particularly grateful for this unpaid work, is enough to dampen any woman's libido.

The unpaid labour of women aged 18–100 is estimated to be worth at least £700 billion to the UK economy, more than five times the value of the financial services industry.

These kinds of inequalities within relationships often lead to the woman being the organiser in the family: the one who reminds you it's your mum's birthday, renews the home insurance and does the grocery shopping. In many ways they take on the more grown-up role in the relationship. Then, somewhere down the line, these same women will be told by their partner of ten years 'you've changed'. Yes, Malcolm, because it's been a literal decade, why haven't you?

Anyone who tries to paint themselves as the victim of being married to a frigid old woman, or the hero because he's staying for the kids (and cheating on their mum in the process), is a special kind of dickhead.

It really says something about male entitlement to the female body that the word 'sexless' is enough to justify breaking your marriage vows. It's 'for better, for worse', Marvin, not 'for better for worse, unless worse means no sex, which is the exception that proves the rule, obvs'.

The openly married people on dating apps will often also say something along the lines of 'don't judge me, you don't know the full story'. And then it turns out the full story is that his wife doesn't want to fuck him anymore. What a harrowing tale, you poor darling.

The silver lining of the above brands of dating app marrieds is that they are easily enough avoided; they literally tell you they're cheating so you can opt out. How gentlemanly of them.

M

The third type are the most slippery, and there is a depressing amount of them out there too. They are the ones who are married or in long-term relationships but *don't* tell you. They'll have you believe you're dating (or fucking) a single dude. They may even make you feel like you might have a future together, when in reality, they have no intention of changing their situation.

This all sucks and unfortunately there is no guaranteed way to avoid them. But there are some tell-tale signs to look out for, and then promptly run away from. You can thank me later.

If the dude has no photos of his face, he may try to convince you that he is a man of mystery. He is not. He is a man of married with kids. He may also say he has no photo 'for work reasons' – this is a crock of shit. Name one workplace that states you can only post pictures of your headless torso on a dating app. Which top-secret accounting firm do you work at, Michael? Because I have it on good authority from someone who used to work at MI5 that *actual spies* have pictures of themselves on their Tinder bios, so I don't see why your middle-management role would need to be shrouded in mystery.

If a cishet man uses the word 'discreet' in reference to the kind of relationship they are looking for, then they might as well run a red flag up the mast as far as I'm concerned. Same goes for 'no-strings fun', especially if they want to have said fun during normal working hours, or at a neutral, private location. They may dress it up as some sort of sexy rendezvous, but it's more likely they don't want to risk being seen with you in public.

The same cynicism should be extended to those who ask to message you on apps where the messages disappear once they're read. Apps like Snapchat, Kik and Viber are perfect for those who want to hide their correspondence (and their unsolicited dick pics). And even if they are using standard messaging like

M

WhatsApp, do they go quiet in the evenings or at the weekends? A lot of cheaters will only text you when they aren't around their live-in partners, so this is something to keep an eye on.

Speaking of live-in partners, I would also steer clear of anyone telling you they still live with their ex 'as friends', 'for financial reasons' or, of course, 'for the kids'. Is it possible that this is a platonic arrangement? Yes, it is. But it's also a very convenient lie that means they don't have to hide things from you, or keep coming up with excuses about why they always stay at yours and never vice versa – another dead giveaway. To be honest, even if it is true and he seems like an amazing guy, I'd tell him to call me once he's moved out; the whole thing sounds messy as fuck.

In an ideal world, the only people on dating apps would be single or in open and polyamorous relationships that they were upfront and honest about. But, alas, we do not live in an ideal world. We live in a world where ageing men are branded as silver foxes while older women are seen as past it. We live in a world where women are told to have babies and then resented for the time and energy they spend raising them. We live in a world where boys are socialised to believe that sex is something that they are entitled to – something women withhold or give freely – and so become men who think not getting any makes infidelity more excusable.

And yes *women cheat too*, I know this! As a feminist I fully believe in women's ability to encompass the whole spectrum of humanity, including being selfish pricks. The clandestine nature of infidelity makes it almost impossible to get airtight data, but studies routinely show that men cheat *more*. Some might put this down to biological urge, I put it down to socialised entitlement. So there.

TL;DR

Married men are not 'forbidden fruit', unless the fruit you're referring to is a forgotten, shrivelled apple at the bottom of the bowl. In other words, don't put them inside you.

N

is for
No Single
Mums

"No single mums."

Translation: I, a grown man who turns his pants inside out to re-wear instead of washing them and doesn't have a bed frame, am pre-emptively rejecting women who run their own household and keep small humans alive. Seems legit.

Would you date a single parent? If your answer is no, fear not, I am not about to spend this entire chapter trying to convince you otherwise. As frustrating as it is for us breeders, there are several valid reasons why someone would not want to date a person who has kids.

There are no valid reasons, however, to write 'no single mums' in your dating bio.

I would argue that no one, parent or not, should date someone with this in their bio. Those three words communicate a contempt for women with children, especially if said women also wish to be seen as desirable, datable beings. I'd go so far as to say that they signal a regressive, misogynistic attitude towards women and relationships.

How do I know this? Well, the less subtle among the 'no single mums' crew reveal it when they follow that phrase with 'if you were such a catch, he wouldn't have left you'. I mean, it's hard to know where to start with that bin fire of a sentence. Do these men really subscribe to the idea that lone mothers are all abandoned by the father of their children? Jilted and alone, awaiting the charity of a man to lift them up out of their hopeless circumstances? The 19th century called, Nigel, and it wants its stereotypes back.

A man who assumes that a woman who has children and isn't in a relationship is somehow of less worth is not a man any woman should want.

If the reason he won't date single mothers is because they have been rejected by the father of their kids, then he sees women's value as explicitly attached to men's approval. It wouldn't even occur to him that it may have been the mother who did the rejecting, or, in the words of comedian Katherine Ryan in her 2019 special *Glitter Room*, 'He left because I asked him to. I asked him more than once!'

This reductive approach also assumes kids = baggage, and having to deal with ex-partners = drama. Because of course the possibility of a mature mutual split hasn't entered their consciousness. They've never had one of those because all of their exes were psychos, after all. What a strange and inexplicable coincidence.

Of course, assumptions about single parents don't only exist in the minds of toxic man-babies.

In fact, if I were to write an Austen-esque satire of my dating history, it would probably begin with the line:

'It is a truth universally acknowledged, that a single woman in possession of a child, must be in want of a stepdad.'

The annoying thing was, that I often wasn't looking for someone to fall for, I was just looking for some fun. Wink wink. But too many men assumed, as soon as they knew I had a kid, that casual dates and sex were off the table. I was obviously on the prowl for a dad replacement.

I remember talking to a guy on Tinder for a while; it was going well and we were planning to meet up. He seemed nice and was in his late thirties so I thought he would be vaguely mature about things, lol. But when I mentioned my son, his response was, 'Oh okay, that's not really what I'm looking for right now.'

What do you mean, Nicholas? You're not looking for a three-year-old boy? I should hope not. He went on to explain, unprompted, that a friend of his had got together with a single mother and 'taken on' her kids, and that that was great for some people but he didn't really think it was for him.

Here was I, quite newly separated. I wanted someone to take me on dates and make me feel nice things; I had no intention of introducing anyone to my son for a very long time. But as soon as I mentioned the existence of offspring, this man thought I was interviewing for stepdads. When I explained this misunderstanding to him he was, at least, self-effacing and said, 'I've shot myself in the foot there, haven't I?' Yes, you have.

As a single mum, dating has often been frustrating and deflating for me. Frequently, prospective partners chose not to date me once they knew about my son. I hated how the knowledge that I had a child seemed to change how some men saw me – from an exciting prospect to a nuclear hazard to be kept at arm's length. I hated the assumptions that were made about me and what I wanted based on this fact alone.

But, with hindsight, I'm glad they bowed out early. I don't want to fall for someone who is uncomfortable with one of the central aspects of my life.

When I told another guy I had a kid, he said he wouldn't be able to meet up for our date after all, because he had to shovel fertiliser into his raised beds. That's right, ladies – don't have kids unless you want to be less desirable than a date with actual dirt.

Still that was better than the man who creepily exclaimed, 'I've never been with a mum before, that's kind of hot.' Dude, think that all the way through and sit with your grossness.

Other mums I know have had comments about breastfeeding and intrusive questions about whether they had a vaginal birth or C-section. The latter was so the guy would know what to expect, down there. It really makes the ones who are simply scared away seem perfectly delightful, doesn't it?

I could sort of forgive younger men for not wanting to get involved with someone who is clearly in a different life stage, but anyone over 35 needs to realise they are ruling out a lot of great people by having a blanket no-kids policy. This applies to all genders really. As I've said, there are good reasons people have not to date parents. Maybe you're looking for something long term and you know you don't want kids to be part of your future; maybe you've dated someone with kids before and losing them as well as your partner in the break-up was too much; maybe you really like taking last-minute holidays and need someone with a flexible schedule. All of this is valid. Basically, as long as your reasons aren't based on knee-jerk reactions or stereotypical assumptions, we're good here.

Having said it applies to all genders, I have to add that the same stigma simply doesn't get applied to single dads as it does single mums. Being a good dad is often seen as an attractive quality, rather than something that's off-putting. In the rare occurrences of men being the main caregiver in a single-parent family, they are often regarded as suburban heroes. Men get credit for 'sticking around' and, you know, continuing to parent their own children after a break-up. They are celebrated for any sign of being domestic or nurturing, while these qualities and skills are simply expected of women.

I guarantee that the men who proclaim in their bio that they want 'no single mums' will still expect their partners to have all of those stereotypical feminine attributes, too. They just want their fertile and caring girlfriend to direct all of her domestic goddess energy into making their lives (and potentially the lives of their future offspring) content. After all, the whole reason they think single mothers ended up that way is because they failed to keep their men happy, right?

Well, wrong, obviously, but you try telling these bellends that. Best to avoid them altogether. Trust me, I'm a mother.

N

Aileen Barratt

TL;DR

Being a single parent is not a failure. Writing 'no single mums' on your dating bio is a major fail.

O
is for
Origins

"What are your origins?"

Translation: I've never asked a white woman this, but if you tell me I'm racist I will be outraged by the accusation.

~~~~~~~

Everyone has been asked where they are from hundreds of times in the course of a getting-to-know-you conversation. If you're racialised as white, however, you're much less likely to have had that question followed up by another one, usually along the lines of 'no but where are you from *originally?*'

As a white woman living in the UK, I have never been asked what my origins are while online dating. Sure, as I get to know someone I'm dating we might start to discuss family history, or they might clock that my name is Irish and ask about that. But I am never interrogated. No one has ever insisted that they know my origins better than I do.

For Women of Colour (WoC), this line of questioning, with all its implied stereotypes and fetishisations, is exhaustingly familiar both on and off the apps.

In 2020 I created a series of translations of the phrase 'what are your origins' with my fellow instagrammer @PizzaSaviour who is a Woman of Colour from London. She, like many of us, has a whole bunch of screenshots of awkward, insulting and downright gross interactions with men on dating apps. The ones she shared with me on this topic involved men's probing questions about where she was from. You know, like *really from*. When she repeatedly told them 'London' or 'I'm British' many of them kept saying things like 'I meant your roots' or 'you don't look British'. Fun times.

When @PizzaSaviour and I came up with the translation for this chapter, we couldn't settle on just one because 'what are your origins' can also mean, for example:

'I don't want to know your origin story, I want you to know that I've noticed you aren't white and maybe fetishise you a bit.'

or

'I am asking this question based entirely on your race, but later on I'll probably tell you that I don't see colour.'

And that's the tip of the iceberg. A whole book couldn't comprehensively cover all of the ways the intersections of racism and sexism affect dating and romance – and even if it could, that book certainly shouldn't be written by me: White Lady™. But this is a book about what dating app language and interactions reveal about modern misogyny, so to omit any discussion of it at all would be to at best ignore and at worst erase the very real experiences of WoC.

Throughout this book I discuss the ways in which misogynistic attitudes see women as less than fully human, how they flatten us from multi-dimensional beings into narrow stereotypes. How much more so, then, is this the case when you are racialised as another marginalised identity?

A lot more.

Some white people have what they describe as 'preferences' for dating certain races. They may see it as a positive or complimentary thing, but most racial preferences are laced with fetishisation and steeped in harmful stereotypes.

Although the perspectives I share in this chapter are mostly about men's attitudes to and interactions with Women of Colour, having a so-called preference for a race outside of your own is not something that is restricted to one gender. So, if any of the following makes you uncomfortable, or reflect on your own dating behaviour, well, good. Lean into that.

In her novel *Queenie*, Candice Carty-Williams brilliantly sketches the dehumanising treatment Black women receive while online dating. The eponymous main character, Queenie, has various relationships and casual sexual encounters with non-Black men, many of whom dehumanise her in the process. In one part of the book some girls at a party sign Queenie up to OKCupid and she receives an influx of fetishising messages

O

including the eloquent opener 'Chocolate girl :)' and the gross declaration that 'I might not be black but trust me you wouldn't know it from my dick'.

Alongside fetishisation, Black women also disproportionately face rejection. Stephanie Yeboah writes in her book *Fattily Ever After* about the ways in which fat Black women specifically, when they aren't being hypersexualised, are 'being portrayed as hypermasculine, or overly maternal and desexualised'. There is very little space for Black women to occupy where the fullness of their humanity is acknowledged and celebrated.

According to 2014 data from the book *Dataclysm*, Black women got on average 75% of the messages women of other races get on dating sites.

European beauty standards still dominate the media and dictate most people's concept of who is beautiful. That means proximity to whiteness = attractiveness in the minds of many, whether they are conscious of it or not.

In *Dataclysm*, Christian Rudder, the founder of OkCupid, demonstrates the racial disparity in dating app matches, which affects Black women more than any other race and gender group. He also shows that when someone adds white as one of their ethnicities (you can choose more than one on OKCupid, so you could be Latino and white, for example), their ratings on the dating app go up. And it's not a handful of super racist dudes skewing the numbers – it's all of us.

Data shows, too, that all races are most likely to match with someone who is in the same race category to them, which

O

makes sense culturally for many people. But it also shows that non-Asian men tend to favour Asian women quite highly. This isn't the compliment it seems on the surface because it is, in part at least, due to the widespread fetishisation of East Asian women.

In a 2021 article for *The Latch*, Vietnamese-Australian writer and activist Alyssa Ho says, 'Racial fetishisation is so much more than just acknowledging someone's race, it's making it the only part of their identity considered. It's when the person with a fetish completely dismisses who a person really is and instead projects their preconceived stereotypes, unrealistic expectations and harmful generalisations onto them.'

As an Asian woman dating in Australia, Ho has experienced firsthand the way these generalisations impact her relationships with men who hold sweeping stereotypes about her race. That's not surprising when the hypersexualisation of East Asian women is ubiquitous in popular culture, as is their depiction as submissive and docile in temperament. It's everywhere from *Madame Butterfly* and *Miss Saigon* to *Memoirs of a Geisha* and the portrayal of Vietnamese and Korean women as sex workers in countless war films that centre the experience of male American soldiers.

Ho writes that she's come across many men who often unashamedly refer to their obsession with Asian women as 'Yellow Fever' and openly speak about 'their love for how "tight" and "promiscuous" Asian women apparently are'. Excuse me while I do a sick in my mouth.

While white women might express shock at these attitudes, I would argue that you can draw a parallel between the fetishisation of Asian women by non-Asian men and the fetishisation of Black men by non-Black women. The hypersexualisation, assumptions about body type and genitalia, and general dehumanisation are all strikingly similar.

O

Sure, this is a book about misogyny, but in a chapter on racism not mentioning the racist ways in which many non-Black (and especially white) women approach sex and dating would frankly feel icky. Many of the stereotypes about Black men's sexual prowess have their roots in rhetoric that dates back to chattel slavery, a time when people from the African diaspora were literally seen as less than human by those racialised as white.

So, if you're a white woman who has had a jolly good time reading through a list of all the ways men can be shitty sexists and now you feel a bit ambushed by the calling out of your own behaviour, well good again! We all have work to do on our biases, so there's something for you to look at, challenge and change.

It's impossible to list all the ways in which WoC can be fetishised in one chapter. The othering romanticisation of non-white women as 'exotic' mingles with colonialist undertones of entitlement and ownership to produce a particularly putrid mix. While the many facets of misogyny detailed in this book still apply whatever your ethnicity, racism compounds the experience. Any man who either fixates on or completely avoids dating certain ethnicities is one to be avoided by all of us.

O

TL;DR

Maybe you have
a preference,
maybe it's racism.

P

is for
Points

"Points if you ..."

Translation: The patriarchy has enabled me to believe that my (masculine) interests and pursuits are superior to your (feminine) interests so I think I am in a position to hand out bonus points to the women of Tinder.

Babe, never pretend to be interested in shit you're not into to impress a man. And don't pretend to not like things you actually enjoy so as not to disappoint him. Your interests are just as valid as those of some dudebro with a vinyl collection.

... drink pints.

... don't spend hours getting ready.

... are a gamer.

Points if you ...

.... like anal.

... can hold your drink.

... listen to Tame Impala.

... are 420 friendly.

... know who Leonard Cohen is.

... have your own eyebrows.

... watch anime.

... know the difference between Marvel and DC.

TL;DR

#JoyBeforeBoys

is for
Quiet

"Does anyone talk on here?"

Translation: I have one chance to sell myself as a potential partner in this bio but instead I'm using that space to complain about the lack of chat.

Online dating is frustrating for a whole host of reasons, and not all of them are misogyny. One pretty universal experience, which seems to happen regardless of gender, is that lots of people you match with just never speak. Either that or you get banal chitchat followed by radio silence.

If this happens to you a lot, don't take it personally. It really is just one of those things. Lots of people swipe for fun or an ego boost, lots of men swipe right on literally everyone and then see who matches, then there are bots, which I don't really understand but they exist and have fake profiles, apparently. It can be disheartening at first but, meh, not everyone wants to talk to you, c'est la vie.

This is not the attitude of disgruntled bio writers though. You know the type I mean, the ones who use most, if not all, of their profile to run through their dislikes and provide a list of complaints about their experience thus far. Because, as we all know, that's super hot.

That was sarcasm.

Statements like 'don't match if you're not going to bother talking' baffle me. I mean, I get the frustration, but what are these dudes hoping to achieve? People who match and don't talk probably aren't paying any attention/don't care what your bio says.

These guys can't see far enough past their own bruised egos to notice that their attitude may be contributing to the lack of interest from women. But that's not their fault, it's obviously ours, okay?

In the end, complaining like this serves only as an indication that you are, to use a technical term, a grumpypants. You're taking something universal personally and having a public strop about it. There seem to be a subsection of men who do this a lot on dating apps. I have chatted with several guys who are convinced 'it's really hard for men on here'. Sure my dude, women get sexually harassed within seconds and verbally abused when we offer the slightest rejection, not to mention fearing for our personal safety when actually going on dates, but you're the ones who are really suffering.

When I have asked men who believe this to explain what they

mean by implying that it is somehow harder for men than it is for women on dating apps, they often offer explanations like 'no one replies'. My insistence that this is something that happens to everyone is rarely taken on board. If you're a misogynist and women don't reply to your messages, it's pretty easy to conclude that it must be because most of us are stuck-up bitches. Poor blokes, eh?

The sentiment that online dating is easier for women that these grumpypants hold doesn't seem to have much to do with the quality of our experience. Rather, that it is easier for us to get matches and maybe dates too. It's a numbers game, and apparently we're winning, which you'd think would feel more fun.

It may be true that women get more matches on average than men do. This is partly due to the fact that, as mentioned previously, many men's entire dating app technique is to swipe right on literally everyone. Women are generally more likely to read bios, and once you've waded through that shit show it's defo gonna narrow down your options.

But also, so what? So what if women get more matches? That doesn't make it hard for men, unless they are entitled pricks who take any rejection as a personal slight … wait, yeah, I see it now.

Whether based on fact or fiction, the idea that it might be easier for women to find dates or even get laid than it is for them absolutely infuriates the modern misogynist. Anger at women's increased sexual agency in choosing partners (and, importantly, in not choosing them) has spawned entire sexist subcultures such as incels and pick-up artists. These men feel they are entitled to our bodies and blame us for the fact that they can't access sex. (I'd argue that their misogynistic views might be their biggest barrier in the dating game, but they won't listen to a feminazi like me so I'll save my breath.)

Of course, not every man who spouts nonsense about it being 'really hard for blokes on Tinder' is an incel, but their basic philosophies aren't a million miles apart. Their so-called plight isn't based on any reality of hardship, but rather what they feel they should have.

There'd be nothing to complain about if they didn't expect every other woman they liked to match them or if they didn't take someone not replying to their messages as a personal affront or if they thought it was okay for a woman to go on a date with them and decide there wasn't a spark there.

But if you feel you're entitled to women's time and their bodies, you're gonna have a big old sulk when you don't get them. And if your self-awareness is lacking enough that you take personally the experiences that literally everyone shares on dating apps – silence, rejection, dates that lead nowhere – you might just be one of those dudes who writes a list of complaints as your bio.

TL;DR

If he uses his dating app bio to complain about women not talking on dating apps, then don't talk to him.

R

is for
Ruin My
Life

"Just looking for someone to ruin my life."

Translation: I mistake volatility for passion, and if that isn't a red flag for you then, honestly, get some therapy.

~~~~~~~

Why do we romanticise dysfunctional relationships? 'Ruin My Life' might be a 2018 Zara Larsson track, but the idea that we hurt the ones we love certainly isn't new.

The love hate relationships many of us see as the height of passion and intense love have been popping up in literature for hundreds of years.

Great love stories all seem to involve turmoil, which is understandable – they are stories. A novel about a functional relationship would be dull as fuck, that's why books and films so often end when the couple finally get together. We want to believe they live happily ever after, but we don't want to watch it.

It's not hard to come up with examples of super unhealthy dynamics being portrayed as the height of romance. Heathcliff in Emily Brontë's *Wuthering Heights* is essentially a vengeful stalker, but he's portrayed as the misunderstood romantic hero of the piece.

Writing dysfunctional male leads must have run in the family, because in Charlotte Brontë's *Jane Eyre*, Mr Rochester is a cold-hearted dickhead who keeps his mentally ill wife in the attic.

Seriously though, were the Brontë sisters okay?

The 20th century is not innocent of shipping couples who are obviously not good for each other, like at all. *Gone With the Wind* is a great example, although the tumultuous relationship between Rhett Butler and Scarlett O'Hara is the least of that film's issues (it's racist as fuck). Then there's the modern tragedy of fiction that is *Fifty Shades of Grey*: the book that launched a thousand fake Doms. I haven't watched the Netflix series *You*, but I hear that a lot of viewers found themselves wanting the stalker to end up in a relationship with his victim. So, that's a lot.

There are plenty of less obvious cases as well. The on-and-off-again romances of '90s sitcoms haven't aged well. Ross and Rachel are a perfect example. He lists her faults, resents her career, cheats on her, is jealous when they're not in a relationship, contrives to have her give up the offer of a dream job, and they end up together! Cos, you know, love!

Rachel should have gone to Paris. That is a hill I am willing to die on.

R

These depictions of so-called romance are everywhere in Western literature and popular culture. We end up craving passion and intensity that is actually incredibly unhealthy. And while the desire to have someone 'ruin your life' isn't inherently misogynistic, we should definitely ask who it serves. Does the stereotype of a tumultuous relationship actually enable abusers?

When we see so many fantasies of love that involve obsessive behaviours, screaming rows and break-up/make-ups, I think it's easier for women, especially young women, to become convinced that men get angry at you because they care. Or even that they hurt you because they love you.

Of course, many abusers rely on their victims believing this narrative, and so much of popular culture helps them do just that. When the intensely jealous and overbearing behaviour of Edward in *Twilight* becomes the model for a devoted boyfriend/husband, what fucking hope is there?

I spoke to Lalalaletmeexplain, social worker, influencer and author of *Block, Delete, Move On*, about how we see love modelled to us and she pointed out that it's not always just in fiction. 'If you grew up with parents who were often fighting, or you had a tumultuous relationship with one or other of your caregivers, then what you see in the media will serve to validate what you have already experienced,' she says. This sort of validation makes it so much harder for young people to recognise unhealthy attachments and behaviours.

Lala goes on: 'If chaotic relationships seem normal to you, you may find that stable and safe relationships feel weird and unfamiliar. I'd always advise people in that situation to seek therapy before you seek any more heartache.'

From the outside, a lot of abusive relationships might look like the classic intense love story. The phrase 'they wind each other up' gets thrown around a lot. Maybe they're always arguing, or they are super intense and never without the other. Maybe they are always breaking up and getting back together. None of these are certain signs of domestic abuse, but as long as we romanticise volatility, abusers can hide behind the guise of twisted romance.

I'm not saying that men who write 'ruin my life' in their bios are all secret vampires or sadist billionaires; most of them aren't that interesting, for a start. But I am wary of this expectation, from all genders, that love involves conflict and pain. Of course it's not all hearts and roses, but the levels of dysfunctional behaviour romanticised in our culture are pretty disturbing, especially when two women a week are being murdered by partners or former partners in the UK alone.

There is another possible translation for 'looking for someone to ruin my life', though, and it's less pseudo-romantic. Some men are simply indicating that they think women are all crazy bitches who cause stress; like we're cute and everything but we are DRAMA. Needless to say, neither interpretation of this stock phrase should be attracting any of us.

R

Tinder Translator

TL;DR

I don't know who needs to hear this, but there is nothing romantic about two people *ruining* each *other's lives.*

S

is for
See What
Happens

"Looking to date and see what happens."

Translation: Looking to go on a few dates and see if sex happens. After that, I'm looking to see if you'll Netflix and chill with me while I offer minimal effort/affection. Theoretically, I may be open to wanting a girlfriend, but she is almost certainly not going to be you.

On some dating apps you can select the kind of thing you're looking for and add it to your profile. Typically, the categories will be 'casual', 'relationship' and 'not sure yet'. I am suspicious of those who pick the third option in the same way I am suspicious of men who say they are 'looking to date and see what happens', or worse, 'have some fun and see what happens'. Not he's-probably-an-axe-murderer suspicious (though you never can tell), more like he's-potentially-a-fuckboy suspicious.

'See what happens' is a stock phrase too ubiquitous to be described as a red flag; perhaps you even have it in your bio. It's often used as a signifier of being easy-breezy, or open to several different types of relationship. I also think it's used, often unconsciously, to indicate that you're one of the Cool Girls. And if you genuinely are up for going with the flow, that's great. But if you write or say that because you think it's what potential partners want to hear, then I'd advise against it. Being what you think they want you to be is never a great long-term strategy.

S is also for serious (thanks for joining me on this episode of *Sesame Street*) and it often turns out that the people who want to just see what happens also aren't looking for anything serious. They are, in effect, hoping that there's lots of fun (aka sex) and not much seriousness (aka emotions and commitment); and if they see the latter happening? They are outta there.

It's fine, by the way, to not want a serious relationship. Beyond fine. But if you know that's what you want, then saying you actually just aren't sure yet is, well, it's a lie. And I think it's often an intentional one. Because if men were to say that they definitely just wanted something casual, a lot of women would immediately take themselves out of the picture. I'm sure the reverse is true too in many cases, but I suspect the decline in women's options for casual sex would be much less drastic.

Men who want you to come along for the ride (pun intended) and see what happens are often looking for more than sex anyway. They are looking for conversation and company and even physical affection. What they want is what sex workers would call 'the girlfriend experience', but they want it for free and for as long as you'll let them have it. I don't think most of them know that's what they want, but if you want someone to spend time and have sex with without making any requirements on you, well then what else would you call it?

S

I asked my Instagram community: If you have dated someone who wanted to just 'see what happens' did it turn out that they actually wanted a relationship in the end? 79% said they didn't.

For some, girlfriend status is reserved for the Margot Robbie lookalike who also loves to play PS5 games and down pints, not for an actual woman who really exists. For others, they may indeed want a girlfriend, but they know pretty soon that it's not going to be you and just … keep dating you anyway. Charming.

Like the lone wolf lads and the NO DRAMA douches, these men all too often baulk at the first sign that you might be an actual fully formed human with wants or needs or emotions. At least, that's what I've found.

After many tries with 'see what happens' and 'not sure yet' men, I had a bit of a break from dating apps because they were making me feel like shit. I realised that I had never taken the time to think about what I actually wanted, and when I did that, I quickly realised that dating to *just see what happens* wasn't it for me. I wanted to date from a place of knowing what I wanted. I have no objections to casual sex, but I found that for me I couldn't do this long-term semi-casual in-a-relationship but-not-actually-official-because-we-are-both-cool-and-chill thing that seems to be expected of us nowadays. (Yes, I am aware I sound like your nan, but nans are great, so there.)

I realised I wanted either one night stands or a relationship, and that this whole wishy-washy 'let's see what happens' just didn't make me happy.

So, when I went back on the apps, I did so knowing I only wanted to date men who knew what they wanted too. I stopped matching

S

Aileen Barratt

with men who selected 'not sure yet' on their dating profile, because I knew it meant one of two things: that they really didn't know what they wanted, or that they knew full well that they didn't want a relationship but also didn't want to put off all the women who *did* want one. These are the guys who will insist it's more fun to just go with the flow; but it's their flow that they are expecting you to go with, and not vice versa.

Suspecting all this, I was very clear with men I chatted to about what I wanted. And their responses were by and large very predictable. Here's how that conversation would typically go:

> So, what are you looking for on here?

> *Ultimately, I want a relationship.*

> k.

> *What are you looking for?*

> Idk, just looking to date and see what happens. I'm a pretty chill guy.

> *Okay, well I'm only looking to date people who also want a relationship.*

> Yeah, I think you're probably a bit serious for me tbh.

Tinder Translator

These men always seemed to think that me saying I wanted a relationship, that that was my goal, was super intense. Often they might say something along the lines of, 'Well, I can't really say what I want yet, we haven't even met.' I'm asking if you're looking for a relationship in general, Samuel, not if you'd like one with me! I'm not suggesting that once we meet up for coffee you'll officially be my boyfriend. Give me strength.

Some men use the word 'serious' as an insult, as if it's the worst thing a woman could possibly be. It sits in opposition to the Cool Girl mould we're supposed to pour ourselves into in order to be desired.

Too many men want their women to be liquid, able to take the shape of any container assigned to them in any given moment. When we are determined to be our solid, whole selves it is, quite frankly, a major buzzkill.

But we are serious. We aren't frivolous little women. If a man tells you you're too serious for him, my advice is to say, 'Yeah, I agree you're too superficial for me.' They will not like this. Knowing what you want from the dating world can feel super intense because it's actually quite rare. We're often asked if we're 'seeing anyone at the moment', not if we *want* to be seeing anyone, or what we want from said relationship. The goal is to be with someone; who that person is, what the relationship looks like and how it feels are almost secondary questions. Except they shouldn't be.

By the time we reach adulthood, most women have been socialised to attach their self-esteem implicitly to the approval of men. Actually, most men have also been socialised to attach their self-esteem to the approval of other men too. The patriarchy is a clever little thing, isn't it?

But if women are, on some level, busy searching for male approval on dating apps, it becomes harder to be discerning (or 'fussy', as it's often described by people who would like the bar for 'good men' to be just above the flames of hell). Because if you're too sure of what you want, you'll probably have to turn a lot of men away. And then where are you going to get that dopamine high of attention and approval from?

Yourself, maybe?

Rather than dating a lot of vague AF men and having mediocre sex, I recommend buying a really great vibrator, or five.

That, and listening to 'Soulmate' by Lizzo on repeat. Ideally you'll enthusiastically sing along to the lyrics 'look up in the mirror like, damn, she the one!' at the top of your voice until you believe it with every fibre of your being, but if you're on the bus or something you can just do that bit in your head. When you know what you want and you know you don't need a man for validation, well, then see what happens!

TL;DR

You can wait around to see what happens, but there won't be a plot twist. He's a fuckboy, not an M. Night Shyamalan movie.

T

is for
Takes Care Of
Themselves

"Looking for someone who takes care of themselves."

Translation: Basically, I want someone who is slim and removes any hair below the eyebrows from their body. I couldn't give a shit about your actual wellbeing. In fact, if you take time out for self-care and set boundaries to protect your mental health, I'll probably have a temper tantrum.

〜〜〜〜〜

Do you take care of yourself? If you've eaten and washed recently then I'd say the answer to that is yes.

Maybe you also earn money, pay your bills and do things that make your body and mind feel good – amazing stuff, I'm proud of you! Though I should probably warn you that these ways of taking care of ourselves will not cut it with most men who use this phrase in their dating app profiles.

What the shallow blokes of Tinder and large swathes of the general population see as taking care of oneself is emphatically not holistic. It is surface level. And primarily it means they want someone who is slim. They might disguise this as saying they want someone who is into exercise, but ask them to choose between a size 8 couch potato and size 18 gym-goer and watch them change their tune.

Fatphobia is rife in our culture, and the assumptions that go along with it mean that many people can't fathom the possibility that you could be a plus-size person *and* someone who takes care of themselves. The stereotypes of gluttony, laziness and more abound, and they have real-life consequences for millions of people who live in bigger bodies, including accessibility issues, medical bias and employment discrimination. That some loser on a dating app doesn't want to date them is among the least of the problems fat folk encounter, but being plus size in these spaces adds another level of exhaustion.

Almost without exception 'looking for someone who takes care of themselves' is just the more socially acceptable way of saying 'no fatties' – a phrase that isn't as rare as you might think in the online dating world either. I hope I don't need to spend any time explaining to you all why no one should be dating anyone who puts *that* in their bio. (It's because they're a prick.)

Of course, the entitled demands made on your appearance don't always stop at weight. No no, many of these men want you to cultivate a certain look. Long, shiny hair – because short hair on a woman is just *wrong*. But also, don't have extensions or take too long doing said hair because that's annoying. Oh, and don't have any hair anywhere else – remove all of it please. Women with hair on their bodies are gross.

That was sarcasm.

Have you ever gone for a wax or any kind of **hair removal** procedure and had a moment of perspective when you suddenly think 'this is fucking weird'? How did we get to a place where it is normal for women (and increasing amounts of men) to pay to go into a small room where a stranger plays plinky-plonky relaxation music and pulls all of your body hair out by its roots?

A note on hair removal

A quick aside here to say that I know a lot of women remove their body hair for all kinds of reasons, and I'd never want to invalidate that. I'm pretty hairy nowadays, but I still shave my armpits. I just think if hairy armpits were the norm in magazines and red carpets, and a full bush was what you usually saw in porn, a lot of people's preferences would likely change. The practice of hair removal and the association with femininity also has a much more troubling history than you might think, rooted in eugenics and the colonial project to construct a system of racial difference that positioned white people as superior. This topic is explored in detail in the excellent book *Plucked: A History of Hair Removal* by Rebecca M. Herzig.

There you are, spreading your own butt cheeks to ensure that every last hair is reached, and for who?

A man who probably doesn't wash his arse properly, let alone wax it.

T

And therein lies the abject audacity of all these 'taking care of yourselves' requirements: there are a significant number of cishet men in this world who cannot take care of their own personal hygiene.

In April 2020, TikToker @CharsGhost went viral with a video where she explained that her 24-year-old boyfriend hadn't been aware that he needed to wash his butt crack (her words, not mine). When she told him you obviously do need to because … poop … he proceeded to text his boys' group chat to check she was correct. Luckily this particular group of bros confirmed that cleaning that area was, in fact, necessary, but that he needed to check is pretty fucking wild.

Despite the horror you or I might feel at the idea of a grown human not cleaning their nether-regions properly (or at all), it is a phenomenon more common than you think. A lot more.

A couple of years back when my page was still relatively small, a follower on Instagram DMed with the revelation that there is an entire subset of men who deliberately don't wipe their bum after going to the toilet, believing it would be 'gay' to touch their own arsehole. I know, right? Imagine having so much internalised homophobia that you'd rather have poo in your pants than be 'considered gay'.

After sharing all this I was flooded with DMs. Some were from women who had been with men who openly refused to wipe their butts, and many, many more had horror stories of the hideous depths of filth they had encountered in their intimate interactions with cis men. I'll spare you the details (thank me later) but the words skid marks, sheets, mouldy and crotch were involved.

T

Tinder Translator

Now, any time I see a man on a dating app asking for someone who takes care of themselves, I can't help but wonder if he has crumbs round his crack.

I have no field research to back this up (thank God) but I suspect there is a significant overlap between the men who want their women to be svelte arm candy and those whose underpants are perpetually stained. I also imagine that, apart from the accessory factor, another function they're looking for in a partner is long-suffering laundress.

The more misogynistic the partner you end up with, the more likely he is to expect you to take on the majority of the domestic load and, if you have kids, childcare responsibilities. And while you look after the household? Well, you'll also be expected to continue looking after yourself.

The opposite of 'taking care of yourself' is having 'let yourself go'. I hate that phrase, but also kind of love it. There are so many misogynistic connotations to someone saying a woman has let herself go (yes, people say it about men too, go and write your own book about that Terry). Women who gain weight; women who stop wearing make-up and high heels; women who let hair grow on their body; women who dress in more comfortable clothing – all of these are often said to have 'let themselves go'.

But letting go can also be an awesome thing. If we put aside for a moment the fact that we might displease the man babies who like pretty shiny things (actually, put them aside permanently if you can), we'll be able to see that.

There are defo parts of myself I've let go in order to, ironically, become more me. Things I have stopped doing because I knew they didn't make me happy; roles I've stopped playing in the lives

T

of people who don't appreciate me. I've let go a lot of harmful thoughts and replaced them with a good dose of self-compassion. Taking care of myself in this way meant a lot of letting go.

I am pretty sure I can trace the beginning of the end of my own marriage to the point at which I started to really love and accept myself. I spent my twenties trying to fit moulds that I kept popping out of, and filing down my edges so I'd be smooth enough to love. Then I went through Compassion Focussed Therapy, which helped me embrace and like my big, spiky self. And I think that made my husband like me less. I think it was threatening to him. The minute I began to really take care of myself, he checked out.

It was either that which signalled the end, or the time he convinced me to see *Batman v Superman* in the cinema – a film so awful it's grounds for divorce in itself.

Unfortunately, too many men are unlikely to take kindly to this type of self-care. Because it is the kind that helps you see your own worth and feel comfortable in your own skin. It is the kind that makes you set boundaries and ask for more. It is the kind that makes you realise you don't want to be with someone whose affection is contingent on your maintaining a certain appearance or being the perfect accessory.

'Oooh, that girl looks good on you Tony, really brings out your testosterone.'

Again, we are back to that pesky request us women are increasingly making to be seen as whole human beings. Honestly, who do we think we are? Men?

T

TL;DR

They don't want us to take care of ourselves, they want us to take care of them ... and be thin.

U

is for
Users

"No users or time-wasters."

Translation: I am so entitled that I think that any woman who talks to me for more than five minutes has to agree to go on a date with me, or she's a time-waster. And any woman who does come on said date and doesn't sleep with me after I've bought her dinner/been nice to her is a user.

~~~~~~

There are a lot of labels men can give women as a punishment for not fucking them: user, time-waster, tease, frigid, vanilla ... Nowhere are these terms thrown about more liberally than on dating apps.

A decade ago, the term 'user' was reserved almost exclusively to refer to someone who used someone else for sex – but that's emphatically not how these men use the term. Quite the opposite: it basically means someone who won't let them do sex to them (and I use that phrasing on purpose; we know that sex with these douches is not going to be a mutually pleasurable experience) even though they made an effort with them in other ways.

As for 'no time-wasters', before I ventured onto Tinder, the only place I had ever seen that phrase was on a used-car website. I suppose it's meant to put off people who aren't serious about buying the car, but even there it felt odd to me. It seemed to imply that there were a subset of people who spent their free time perusing second-hand vehicles for fun. Maybe there are, but it seems more likely to me that there are lots of people who see a car in real life and don't want it anymore.

The same could be said for women dating men online. Maybe there are a few who think a free drink is worth sitting in the company of any man for an evening, but generally there are a lot more who – and this is gonna sound crazy – want to chat a bit and then meet in person before they decide whether or not they are going to sleep with them. I know, we're such a bunch of divas!

I get the sentiment of not wanting to spend hours talking to someone and then it going nowhere. The whole 'not looking for a pen pal' line is relatable – though a grumpy and misguided addition to a dating bio. There were a few times when I chatted to guys for ages only to realise that we were never gonna meet up. It was super disappointing and I was too naïve back then to console myself with the fact that they were probably in a monogamous relationship and getting an ego boost from my attention. Oops.

U

I also really understand that sometimes you can be excited about someone when chatting online and then meet them and be like ... oh no. It's not even necessarily a matter of them not looking like their pictures. They could be exactly as you expected physically but somehow just not. When we're messaging, we have time to think about our replies and portray our personality however we want, but this means that our in-person selves don't always match up. I actually started meeting up with people relatively quickly after a while because I'd built too many men up in my head to be *amazing* before meeting in person and realising that they certainly were not the one for me.

Unlike me, the Entitled Men of Tinder™ couldn't just reflect on what they want and adjust their own expectations and behaviour accordingly. Oh no. It is you, ladies, who need to do that. Only feel safe meeting a man after you've gotten to know him by chatting online? You're a time-waster! Think you have the right to go on several dates and *still* not sleep with the man you've spent upwards of six hours with? User!

I mean, do men really think women are doing this en masse? Choosing to spend our evenings in their company for a couple of glasses of Pinot and some dough balls at Pizza Express? When we could be watching Netflix and not having to make conversation with a bellend?

If you give most women the choice between instant noodles in the comfort of their own home and a free three-course meal in bad company, they'll choose the noodles.

U

Aileen Barratt

Am I saying a woman has never gone on a date with a man for a free dinner? No I'm not, I am well aware of this as a thing that happens, but I think it happens much less than men who call women users or, indeed, gold diggers, think it does.

When I asked my followers if they had ever been on a date just for the free food or drink, only 11% of women said they had.

To be honest I don't have a particular stance on who pays on a date, I'm not sure it matters too much in the grand scheme of things. Some will try to the justify the man paying on the first date (and beyond) by referencing the gender pay gap, but I don't think it's particularly feminist or anti-feminist to allow a man to buy you a meal – macro-economics aside.

There are lots of men who pay on a first date because they think it's a nice thing to do, and it is. There are also lots that pointedly make sure you get the second round of drinks. I remember one guy saying 'it's your round' and looking smug, like he was catching me out. I was like, yeah it is, Uriah, what are you having?

He may have been checking I wasn't a user. But I didn't sleep with him so he defo went home thinking I was a time-waster.

Then there are the men that pay for things because they believe they are engaging in some sort of transaction. That if a woman accepts some drinks or a meal from them then that means they get to have sex with said woman. Usually, a bit of free food is the least you should expect as compensation for enduring the presence of these misogynists for more than a minute. But still, when you say 'thanks, it was nice to meet you, but there wasn't a spark for me', they'll chalk you up as a shallow user.

U

Which is pretty fucking ironic.

Because, in a scenario where men resent you not opening your legs at the end of a date, or even deciding you'd rather not meet up at all after a bit of a chat, who is the actual user? It seems quite clear to me that there is one particular use these men have for women, and it's not particularly wholesome. Calling someone a user because they didn't eventually put out (I hate that term but it feels like one these kinds of men might employ) speaks of the kind of sexual entitlement that underpins rape culture.

No one deserves sex from anyone else, not if they've paid for their drinks, not if they've bought them flowers every day for a year, not even if they fucking married them.

So never let a man make you feel like you owe him sex, or you've led him on. They have imagined this whole deal, you never agreed to it, and frankly even if you did, you have the right to change your mind. That doesn't make you a user, it makes you an autonomous human being. And, frankly, it's your autonomy that makes them so angry. Sucks to be them, I guess.

U

Aileen Barratt

TL;DR

A bottle of prosecco and two hours of their attention doesn't entitle anyone to your body.

V

is for
Vanilla

"Not looking for anyone vanilla."

Translation: I shame women into sex acts they aren't comfortable with.

'Vanilla', a word that I'd mostly heard in reference to ice cream until five years ago, is now the new 'frigid'. And we really didn't need a new one of those.

Much like kink, Dom and choking, vanilla is a term that has made its way into the mainstream from the BDSM community and taken on a horrifying life of its own. In the spaces it originated in, vanilla isn't a value judgement, neither is it something a person can be. It's just a description of what a culture would consider standard or conventional sexual practice.

Some people's tastes may be more vanilla than others, some acts may be considered vanilla, but it's not a measure of how exciting you are or aren't in the bedroom.

Out in the mainstream online world though, from Tinder to TikTok, vanilla has become a badge of shame for those who don't want to engage in certain sex acts – most of which are painful or degrading. *A girl who doesn't like anal? God, she's so vanilla.* In this new context, vanilla has come to mean boring and, therefore, unattractive. The consequences of this are pretty heartbreaking.

'Frigid' was the word bandied about when I was a teenager. And forgive me Gen Z, because I'm going to sound like the mum that I am for a minute. Back then a girl (and it was always a girl) was called frigid if she didn't want to kiss a boy, or if she *only* wanted to kiss and wouldn't 'let him' finger her. Vom. Maybe on a rare occasion it might refer to her not wanting to have penetrative sex, but that was as far as it went. It was never about the *kind* of sex she did or didn't want to have.

The word 'vanilla' is used in just as gendered a way as frigid used to be. I have never heard a man referred to as being vanilla for not wanting to be pegged, for example. This is largely because

men's sexual autonomy is taken for granted. Of course they are subjected to expectations and pressures to perform in the bedroom, but they are allowed to perform as they like; they aren't expected to cater to their partners' tastes in the same way women are – that is not what makes them good at sex.

(Just an aside here to say that catering to your partner's tastes and pleasure, while communicating your own, absolutely is what makes everyone good at sex. In case there was any doubt. Cool? Cool.)

Find yourself in the wrong corner of TikTok in 2022 and you'll be shown a collection of men in their late teens and early twenties making various references to how they'd *never* sleep with a vanilla girl. It's all 'when she says she doesn't like to be choked' and a video of them leaving the room. Okay dude, tell me you can't get hard without hurting a woman without telling me you can't get hard without hurting a woman.

I asked my Instagram community if they had ever been called 'vanilla' because they didn't want to do something sexually. 39% said they had.

Terrifyingly, vanilla (in the context of TikTok douchebags anyway) now means not wanting to be strangled, spat at, hit, treated roughly, etc. Younger women and girls are being taught that's what good sex is. Or at least, that's the kind of sex that boys want, so it's the kind they should be having. Hence the thousands of young women and teenage girls writing comments and dueting fuckboy TikToks saying that they're not vanilla and those girls who are 'are so boring'.

V

There is a time and place to explore your kinks but, fucking hell, it is not with some 20-year-old lad who doesn't know his arse from your clitoris and has himself had his ideas of pleasure imposed on him by the grossness that is Pornhub's home page. Besides, how do you know you're kinky if you've never explored anything else?

Much like the ice cream, vanilla sex may have a rep for being boring but, if you do it right, it'll be some of the best sex you'll ever have. Because, again, all it means is not BDSM – it doesn't mean not exciting.

Vanilla sex could be your partner going down on you until your toes are curling and your vision blurs. It could be spending ages exploring each other with hands and lips. It could be being so desperate for each other you end up fucking on the stairs, not even making it to the bedroom.

Or it could be a highly satisfying session of missionary, that much maligned and, I would argue, often excellent sexual position.

In the reality series *Love Island UK*, there is always an episode where the couples have to play that 'how well do you know your partner' challenge. One of the questions they are asked is, 'What's your favourite sexual position?' A classic of the genre. I'm always a bit cynical of their answers – they are inevitably going to be performative, either for the viewers or who it is they're trying to attract.

Half of the boys always choose 'doggy', which is fine, I guess. I'm not a fan of how many men want to fuck us without having to look at our faces on regular basis, but that's just me.

When women on the show pick supposedly exciting positions (the ones the boys like), such as doggy or reverse cowgirl, the absolute lads do a little cheer. I find this gross. On the 2021 series of the show, two of the women said their favourite position was missionary. In response to this a male contestant said, under his breath, 'A lot of girls here like boring sex.' I also found that gross.

Anyone who thinks missionary is inherently boring makes me sad for them and their sexual partners. Like, are we even thinking of the same thing? Face to face, almost the whole of your bodies touching? Looking each other in the eyes, legs intertwined? That missionary?

If it's not your preference that's obviously fine, but it's not boring.

The thing is that no kind of sex is inherently boring, and all kinds of sex can be. Whether you're in missionary position on a bed or tied upside-down on a rack legs akimbo, things can get mechanical and unexciting. I think it's pretty boring the amount of cishet men who want to have the same kind of sex all the fucking time – sex that just happens to imitate mainstream porn. I mean, where's your imagination fellas, mix it up a bit, stop being so vanilla!

V

TL;DR

Vanilla isn't boring;
it's fucking delicious.

W

is for
Where Are All
The Normal
Girls

"Where are all the normal girls?"

Translation: I am the centre of my own universe to such an extent that I label any woman who doesn't behave exactly how I want her to as abnormal.

What must your concept of a 'normal woman' be if you think there are none on dating apps?

When men say this, they almost always mean they aren't finding women who fit into their criteria of what a 'normal woman' *should* be. They may as well be saying 'where are all the passive and compliant women?' Because that's what they're looking for. They have very little idea of what a normal woman is because, and hear me out here, they haven't ever really paid attention to one.

It's pretty wild how easy it is for men to get through life without ever really taking an interest in any of the women around them. And I mean a real interest, in their personalities, likes, dislikes, hopes, fears and – dare I say it – opinions. That's why it feels so special when you go on a date with a man who asks questions and listens to your answers. That's why it's super sexy when you feel like a man finds you interesting beyond your appearance and surface-level chat.

Have I mentioned at all that the bar is low?

Alas, for too many men their idea of a 'normal woman', and by this logic what a woman should be, has largely been constructed from media messaging and the opinions of other men. Which most of the time are one and the same thing.

The Bechdel Test – so named after Alison Bechdel, the cartoonist whose comic it first appeared in – is a basic principle that measures the representation of women in film. A movie passes the test if it meets three criteria: there are two women characters; the women talk to each other; their conversation is about something other than a man or men. Think about your favourite childhood film, or the films that were popular during your teens: how many would pass this very basic test?

Even today, there are too few films in which the women characters are drawn with as much detail and nuance as the men. Too often, even featured female characters are all style and no substance. To illustrate this, comic writer Kelly Sue DeConnick came up with another test: the sexy lamp test. 'If you can remove a female character from your plot and replace her with a sexy lamp and your story still works, you're a hack.'

Seeing as we tend to socialise along binary gender lines as children and into adulthood, it tracks that a lot of men have never gotten to know a 'normal' woman outside a familial, romantic or

sexual relationship. They get their ideas of what we are and what we're like from TV and films, where women are frequently only relevant in their relation to men and/or for their smoking hotness. When these men do get to know an actual woman and find out we aren't just sexy lamps, it's a bit of a shock to the system. And none of this is helped by the fact that women and girls are basically taught to act like sexy lamps in order to attract a nice man. Or, really, any man. #goals

The Cool Girl is basically a sexy lamp. Stands around looking good? Check. Has no opinions? Check. Shines a light on you without asking for anything in return? Check!

And isn't that what a lot of us tried to be in our early relationships? Perhaps you're still trying to be that. If so, I empathise, but – and I say this with all the love in the world – cut it the fuck out.

Trying to be what some men imagine as a 'normal girl' is an unsustainable feat. You might manage it for years, but eventually you'll start being more you. And he won't like that. Worse than that, by dimming your own light or shining it all on him, you'll never feel seen or loved as the whole person you are. And that shit is soul destroying, trust me.

This might sound all a little extreme, but I think it's a very common dynamic in heterosexual relationships. It never fails to amaze me how many men don't seem to really know much about the women they are married to.

Feminist and author Clementine Ford articulates this perfectly when she suggests that if you want to see whether a man has ever really paid his wife any attention, ask him what he knows about her. If you ask him what he loves about her, Ford explains, he will likely list only things that relate to himself. She's a great mum, she's a great cook, maybe she even makes him laugh and he enjoys her company. But outside of that, what does he know about her? What are her dreams? What does she love to do? That knowledge can be strikingly non-existent, or at least a bit rusty (maybe he paid attention for the first few years).

I think if you'd have asked my husband what he knew about me just before our marriage broke down he could have given a detailed enough answer – the information would have just been six years out of date.

I'm not sure what any of these men are really asking for is 'normal'. I think they mean non-disruptive, undemanding, sexy lamp.

There is, of course, no such thing as normal. Its very concept is underpinned by cultural controls. Those in power dictate what is the norm or the default, so in Western society that is white, cis, straight, non-disabled men. In order to be normal, the rest of us must do our best to be as close to and non-disruptive of that default.

That proximity to 'normal' is infinitely easier to achieve as a cis white woman than, say, a Black trans, non-binary person. My ability to achieve 'normal', however oppressive it may feel, is much more viable, and that's something that I am acutely aware of. But as long as we're trying to be 'normal' as defined by rich white dudes (i.e. the ones that own news channels and movie studios), none of us will ever be truly liberated.

Anyone who has ever pushed back on the norm has been quickly labelled a weirdo, an outcast or even unnatural. Those who brand us with these labels are almost always scared that we're discovering our power.

The men who want 'normal girls' may not know they are scared of strong, decisive, disruptive women, but they are. So, they try to control us by labelling our behaviour as abnormal. The thing is, though, we're onto them. Unlucky, lads.

TL;DR

He says 'abnormal', we say 'has a personality and free will'.

X

is for
Crazy eXes

"All my exes are psychos!"

Translation: I have literally driven several women mad. Run in the opposite direction.

The same men that will demand you be 'normal' are often the ones who will proceed to tell you how 'crazy' *every woman they've ever dated* was. They think there are no normal women in the world because everyone they've ever dated was a psycho. Honestly, I cannot wave the red flags high enough on this one.

What an odd coincidence that all of the women you date turn out to be irrational/insecure/needy/distrusting. It's, like, for sure definitely a coincidence. Not at all representative of a) your attitude to women, and b) your consistent ability to fuck them up.

That was sarcasm.

We have already talked about the way that lots of men make women feel irrational and dramatic. Many of the NO DRAMA crew would definitely describe their exes as psychos for normal behaviour like sometimes getting upset or asking for relationship progression. They'll often follow up their stories of the totally unpsychopathic behaviour with a casual 'I'm glad you're not like that though, you're chill'.

In the midst of a new crush, we can all fail to hear the alarm bells ringing and choose only to listen to the approval of the boy we like. But, if it's not clear, we should really be listening to those bells because if he's telling you his ex was a psycho, him turning out to be a dismissive prick who lacks emotional depth is probably the best case scenario.

There is also the distinct possibility that these men have manipulated and abused their former partners, thus causing the behaviour that they would label as 'psycho'.

Habitual **abusers** often tell their potential victims how horrible/irrational their former partners were. That way, if you get wind of anything negative about those relationships, you're already prepped with the abuser's spin on the situation.

X

Tinder Translator

A note on domestic abuse

There are lots of early warning signs for domestic abuse, and the sooner you get out the better. Talking to friends and family about what's going on can be helpful to get some perspective and prevent you from being isolated. Lalalaletmeexplain's *Block, Delete, Move On* is a great resource to help you spot red flags too. If you are worried or in a situation you are unsure of, please seek professional help. If you feel safe to do so, Googling 'domestic abuse support' and the name of your local area is a good way to find help near you.

It's possible that a man has had a shitty or even abusive ex, of course it is. But if they are divulging lots of details about that right at the start of dating, it should give you pause. Either he has a lot of healing to do, or he's making sure you know his version of events from the get-go.

I've dated a few men who really did have awfully stressful relationships and/or break-ups, but I only found this out in the natural getting-to-know-you part of the relationship where you begin to disclose the more vulnerable parts of your personal history. Healthy people don't lead with 'my ex was a psycho'.

It's also really telling that most of the time these guys are not just talking about one ex. This begs the question, who was the common denominator in all those relationships? And if the women started out 'normal' and ended up as apparent nutters, maybe that common denominator was more than a coincidence.

Men who describe women they're dating, or have dated, as being psychos are sometimes doing so to be deliberately manipulative.

X

Aileen Barratt

189

One sure way to gain control over a person is to make them feel like they're going mad, to convince them that their natural human tendency to have emotions is dramatic. To make them lose their sense of self and question their own judgement. And men have been doing just that to women for centuries.

The term 'gaslighting' gets over-used online, but it originates from the 1944 film of the same name, in which a husband manipulates his wife into thinking she's going mad. Among other things, he makes her believe she is imagining the gaslights dimming, when he is actually turning them down himself. The whole thing is a master class in coercive control.

Gaslighting, then, is a devastating abuse tactic that leaves victims not trusting themselves or their own sense of reality. This then isolates them and leaves them more dependent on their abuser.

Not every man who flippantly bad-mouths his exes by calling them psychos is going to be an abuser. Most of them are just going to be emotionally immature pricks who aren't worth your time. But the risk is there. And there is no reasonable explanation for using that kind of terminology, no version of the psycho-exes bloke you should want to date. So, I say swipe left and save yourself.

TL;DR

Nothing quite says 'I hate women' like a man who refers to all of his previous intimate partners as psychos.

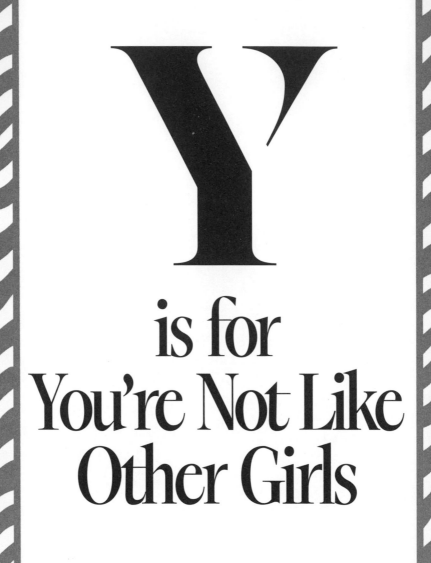

Y is for You're Not Like Other Girls

"You're not like other girls."

Translation: I've just basically said I'm not a big fan of women in general, but you're pretty nice, and I expect you to take that as a compliment.

How many times have you been told, in one way or another, that 'you're not like other girls'? And how many times have you got all excited because, like, that is such a big compliment?

I'll answer first: too fucking many.

It's not always stated in those exact words. Sometimes it's 'you're so interesting to talk to' or 'it's so refreshing how laid back you are' or 'wow, not a lot of girls like *Rick and Morty*'. Sometimes it's even 'God, my exes were such psychos, so glad you're not like that!' What's that, a bunch of red flags, for me?

The patriarchy mainlines misogyny into our veins from such a young age that by our teens most girls won't think twice about taking 'you're not like other girls' as a compliment. And a big one at that. Who cares if all the best people I know are other girls? Right now there's a 17-year-old with cider breath who wants to put his tongue down my throat, so I am going to listen to what he says, thank you very much!

I didn't even lack a basic awareness of feminism as a child and young woman. Seriously, at age two, I was refusing to build a snowman – it was a snowgirl and I'd hear no more about it. I have always been staunchly pro-woman. By secondary school, if a boy had said to me, 'I think most girls are shit, but you're pretty cool,' I would have told him he was being a sexist pig.

Or at least I hope I would have. I probably would have still let him kiss me after, if I'm being totally honest.

Still, yearning to not be like other girls – and so to be special to boys – was very much underneath the surface. That's why they call it *internalised* misogyny.

Despite growing up in a post–Spice Girls 'if you wanna be my lover, you gotta get with my friends' era, I was very much more concerned with securing the lover than enjoying the friends. The male gaze was a light bulb, and I was a little fly constantly buzzing against it, getting burned and then coming back for more. Weren't we all?

Meanwhile, were boys all focussed on the approval of girls? Was their self-esteem totally dependent on our attention? Like fuck it was. Boys were also being taught that it was boys who they needed to impress. Even their pursuit of girls was all too often wound up in their endeavours to prove their worth to their (male) mates. So, that's fun and fulfilling for all concerned.

The world tries ludicrously hard to convince us that being the best *girl*, rather than the best person or simply the best version of ourselves, is what we should strive to be. I suppose it distracts us from realising that we're already better than a lot of men, which would be a disaster for the whole patriarchy thing.

It's also a useful distraction from how fucking sublime other girls really are. Women are my fortress and my inspiration. Women built and sustain me. Almost all of the most constant, nurturing and joyous figures in my life have been women. The majority of music, art and literature that has shaped me was forged from the souls of wonder women.

It really shows how little attention these men have paid to women, that they actually think *not* being like them is a compliment. It really shows how brainwashed women have been that so many of us have taken it as such.

If I'm not like other girls, then what am I like? Cishet men? No thanks.

But isn't that what these men are saying, most of the time? *You're kind of like a dude, but also you're a girl so we can do sex without compromising my toxic masculinity.* Or maybe not, maybe it's that you're more like the fantasy Cool Girl they've read so much about. Either way, it's not really you they're talking about; it's what they want you to be, for them.

Y

Aileen Barratt

Maybe you have the same interests as him and he thinks that's unusual for a girl. Maybe you make him laugh so he thinks you're funny for a girl. Maybe you're okay with keeping things casual so he thinks you're cool for a girl. Maybe you're engaging to debate with about subjects that he's interested in, so he thinks you're really smart, *for a girl*. Urgh.

If it's not clear by now, let me make it so: none of us should be happy with any so-called compliment that ends with *for a girl*.

Knowingly or not, this form of 'praise' has always been a method of control. A stamp of approval from the men whose love we are told completes us. And a way of separating us off from our allies, our sisters, our biggest cheerleaders and closest friends. In a strange way, it is telling us to be less like ourselves.

The idea that being remarkable or hilarious or cool or bright or strong has anything to do with other women *not* being remarkable or hilarious or cool or bright or strong is the biggest pile of shit I've ever heard. Personally, I know I am those things *because* of other women, not in spite of them.

Other girls are funny and talented and brave and beautiful. They are sharp and sexy and fragile and smart. They are strong and bold and sometimes troubled. They are magnificent and multifaceted. They are matriarchs and misfits. They are powerful and vulnerable and courageous and kind. They are warrior women and I hope to God that I am like them!

Y

Tinder Translator

TL;DR

Actually, I am like
other girls, thank
you very much.

Z

is for

ZZZZZ

ZZZZ Z ZZZZZ ZZZZZ ZZZZZZZ

No translation for this chapter, but I'm determined to crowbar a tenuous Z in here somehow! Over the last 25 chapters, we've explored the misogynistic double speak that pervades the experiences of women on dating apps and beyond. And you know what? All that can be really fucking exhausting to navigate. So, I didn't want to finish this book without explicitly saying: you can take a break. You might want a relationship, but you *don't need one*. And if dating is taking more from you than it's giving, you can stop for a bit. Date yourself, or just like, rest, you know? You deserve it.

ZZZZZZZ ZZZZZZZ ZZZZZ ZZZZZ

Conclusion

Raise the Bar!

It's easy to get jaded among the relentless misogyny that bombards anyone trying to find a nice man to date in haystack full of dating app douchebags. Many of us even come to accept it as just the way it is, which can lead to lowering our standards, or pretending to ourselves we don't have any, in order to go on dating.

The bar is low when it comes to what constitutes a 'good' man and a 'good' relationship, and that can lead to some of us feeling we're being too fussy, too demanding, too much in general. Plenty of men love to make us feel that way, too. The bar being low serves the pondscum of the dating pool very well.

For those who have partners, the general state of dating can mean we end up feeling grateful for a man who replies to texts or remembers our birthday or … wipes his arse. Simply not being a misogynist becomes worthy of praise when sexism greets us at every turn.

But I am here to tell you that the bar being generally subterranean doesn't mean yours has to be. You can decide exactly what you want, and not settle for any other nonsense. In a relationship this might look like stating your needs and asserting your right to live fully as yourself. And as a single person, knowing what you want can make the whole dating process feel a bit less like swimming through raw sewage.

For my birthday a few years ago, I got a 'style profile' at a department store. It was basically a consultation that told me what colours and shapes of clothing suited me. It was great, and it made me a much more efficient, less emotional shopper. I'd look at a pretty piece of clothing and think, 'That's nice, but it won't look good on me.' Not because I can't look good, or because it wouldn't look good on someone else – just because I knew what suited me, and that wasn't it. It saved me from many crestfallen moments, staring into poorly lit three-way mirrors in changing rooms feeling shit because I tried something on that wasn't meant for me. I stopped giving clothes the power to make me feel bad just because not every garment made me feel good.

This is how I started to feel about online dating once I had a clear sense of a) my own value, and b) what it was I actually wanted. I didn't take it personally when dudebros told me I was too serious, and I didn't even entertain dating men who weren't sure if they wanted a relationship. I was sure, and it was nothing personal, I just didn't have time to faff around.

Raising your standards and sticking to them involves a little bit of bravery in a world that tells women we aren't complete without the love of a man. This kind of thinking traps some women in unfulfilling relationships and makes others feel like they should go on underwhelming dates. Whenever I talk about raising the bar and not settling, I always get responses along the lines of 'but what if I keep my high standards and don't find anyone who meets them?'

My response is always the same: think that question all the way through. Is what they are saying that they're so worried about having no boyfriend, that they'd rather have one that isn't right for them than none at all? Because the answer to 'what if I don't meet anyone who can get over the bar I set?' is that you'll be single. Maybe for a long time. And that's okay. It's more than okay, because you are enough. And, in the words of the late great Whitney Houston: 'I'd rather be alone than unhappy.'

I suppose my point is, despite spending a whole book lamenting the many ways in which misogyny abounds in the world of dating apps and beyond, it's not something that we have to accept or play along with. Quite the opposite. In fact, I think half of these men are so disgruntled because a lot of us are sick of playing along, which is incredibly frustrating to some who think they're entitled to our time and bodies.

If you're sick of playing along too, you can just stop. You don't have to follow the unwritten rules of dating because 'that's just how things are', you don't have to entertain fuckery because 'at least he's honest', you don't have to do anything you don't want to do. The literal worst that can happen is that you'll remain single, and that, my friend, is not a disaster, whatever you might have been told.

Regardless of our relationship status, the patriarchy would like us to be grateful for the crumbs of goodness men throw to us. It would like us to be passive, or even affirming, when we hear phrases like those listed throughout this book. It doesn't want us to think things all the way through because when we do, we see all the subtle ways sexism is woven into our everyday interactions. And that makes the misogynists nervous.

The threat of rejection hangs over all women when we begin to consistently challenge the ways the world would like us to be smaller and softer. We will be portrayed as a broken record, a feminist killjoy, a total drag. This threat is compounded if your other identities intersect to further deny you a seat at the table. But fuck that table! The seats are uncomfortable and most of the other people around it are insufferable rich white dudes.

Being fully ourselves can be magical but it's fucking scary too. Maybe fewer people will like you, maybe fewer men will want to date you. But guess what? The people who do like you will actually like _you_.

Not some streamlined, sexy-lamp version of yourself you've been unconsciously cultivating since you were 12. You. The woman you worry talks too much or is too big or too critical or too messy or too … you. And that's a little revolution right there.

It took me a long time to see how much the expectations of men who weren't interested in knowing me fully had restricted my self-expression. Like many women I was an excellent contortionist, bending myself to fit into a box I was too big for. It was never sustainable; eventually an ungainly limb would pop out and ruin the illusion. And I would feel like that was my fault. When I started blaming the box instead of myself, the whole world looked different.

My hope is that this book has helped you see the box more clearly too, and that it will empower you to unfurl yourself a bit more. To stretch out and take up space you've been told isn't yours. Maybe you'll use your newly free limbs to eat cake with both hands, or throw joyous shapes on the dance floor, or hail a taxi and drive off into a fabulously fuckboy-free sunset.

Misogyny seeks to rob women of our full humanity; the patriarchy uses our less-than status to control us. But we're onto it now, and that means we don't have to play along. You don't have to play up to expectations or play down your worth. Because you are always enough, and you'll never be too much for the people who will love you right.

Go and follow

This book has been made richer and more rounded by much of what I've learned from other writers and creators on Instagram. Social media should never be the only place you learn more about the world, but it's a good place to start. This little list is a – very much non-exhaustive – selection of Instagram accounts I highly recommend.

@AlliraPotter beauty, body positivity and life-affirming 'wild and witchy' shit

@AlokVMenon a radically loving invitation to reject the gender binary (and some kickass outfits)

@AlyssaHoWritings Vietnamese-Australian writer and anti-racism advocate

@BobbiLockyer Aboriginal artist, designer and photographer bringing beauty to your feed

@TheBodzilla body acceptance, fat positivity, incredible outfits and effulgent joy

@BrandonKyleGoodman blesses us with Messy Mondays, unabashed wisdom and queer Black joy

@CarlyFindlay appearance and disability activist, speaking truth to power

@CathyReayWrites disability justice, polyamory and queerness, single motherhood and skincare!

@TheChronicIconic in her own words, an 'Autistic, Mad, Cripfluencer™ Jewess'

@Clementine_Ford eviscerating feminist analysis delivered by your favourite Big Sister

@Farida.D.Author feminist author informed by her lived experience in Arab culture

@galdemzine committed to sharing perspectives of people of colour and marginalised genders

@HabenGirma human rights lawyer advancing disability justice

@Kelechnekoff razor-sharp takes and incisive wit – nobody tweets like Kelechi

@LaLaLaLetMeExplain qualified social worker, sex and relationships educator and anti-fuckboy warrior

@Nina_Tame clear, candid content on the joys of disability and the downfalls of ableism

@RichieReseda insights on abolitionism and dismantling the patriarchy

@RubyRare sex-positive educational content paired with brightly coloured queer joy content

@SalmaElWardany poetry, sharp-witted feminism and cathartic lessons for #notallmen

@ScottyUnfamous fabulous, glamourous delivery of the sex education you did not get in school

@TheSexDoctor sex science insight that you can apply to your life

@StephanieYeboah beauty, plus-size fashion, fat positivity and plenty of Black girl magic

@ThirtySomethingSingle diverse dives into dating, fatphobia, sex positivity and the occasional bit of radical theology

@WeAreManEnough undefining masculinity and freeing us all from patriarchy

Go and read

Here is a selection of books – some I've referenced in this book, others that have shaped my thinking and that I recommend.

All About Love by bell hooks

Block, Delete, Move On by Lalalaletmeexplain

Boys Will Be Boys by Clementine Ford

Dataclysm by Christian Rudder

Fattily Ever After by Stephanie Yeboah

Fight Like A Girl by Clementine Ford

Gone Girl by Gillian Flynn

I Am Not Your Baby Mother by Candice Brathwaite

Mediocre by Ijeoma Oluo

Men Who Hate Women by Laura Bates

Plucked by Rebecca M. Herzig

Queenie by Candice Carty-Williams

Rage Becomes Her by Soraya Chemaly

What White People Can Do Next by Emma Dabiri

Your Silence Will Not Protect You by Audre Lorde

Acknowledgements

This book was made possible as a direct result of the community that has surrounded, supported, shared and 'liked' me on Instagram. So, if you're one of those people, I'd like to thank you, seriously, because you've changed my life.

To my Patreon subscribers: you paid me for my work, and in this shitty capitalist world where things cost money, that means a fuck load. Many of you have been subscribers from way before I had a big page or a book deal. This was transformational for me – it meant I could spend time thinking and creating. I love you guys. Shout out to the insta-sanctum!

Special mention to my patron and absolute angel Jane McTaggart. Thank you for your generosity and insights over the past two years.

There are so many women whose support and championing of me has led me here too. Lalalaletmeexplain, thanks for sharing my page when it was tiny-small, but more so for being my internet friend, contributing to this book and giving me so much insight into the publishing process. Sophie Milner, you are an amazing cheerleader and general babe, I'm so glad we cyber-met (and then real met), thank you. Kate, have loved our chats and growing our pages/developing our approaches together. Clementine Ford, what can I say? Thank you for becoming a most excellent friend and champion, and introducing me to so many Aussie babes, including …

Jacinta di Mase, my agent. A thousand thank yous! You saw the potential for this book before anyone else and helped me make it happen. So glad you slid into my DMs.

Alice, Emily, Rochelle and all at Hardie Grant Books, thank you for taking a punt on my idea and guiding me to a place where it's an actual real-life book. Alissa for making the book look pretty and bearing with my seven thousand notes. Isabella for hooking me up with all the marvellous publicity. What an absolute pleasure to work with you all this has been.

Natel Allen, thanks for your thoughts on the world of being an 'entrepreneur'. Sasha Rosenberg, for your encouragement and help with Chapter O. I dream of a future where you're no longer interrogated by mediocre dudebros as to where you're *really* from. Cathy Reay, thanks for challenging me to include ableism in my understanding of the intersectional aspects of dating. Sasha (@MindYourOwnPlants), thanks for being my fabulous sensitivity reader and giving me the insight of your lived experience – it makes the book all the richer. Stephanie Yeboah, thank you for the words of encouragement and support.

To my family. Mum, for raising me in a feminist household and dropping wisdom in such an offhand way that you forget you've said it. Dad, for encouraging me so much with my writing and telling me how brilliant I am – not everyone gets those reminders! Elliott, for being as shit as me at replying to texts but always having my back too – love you bro.

To my son, who gives me hope for the future, who is funny and kind and sensitive. You're the joy of my life.

To Chris, my proofreader, cheerleader and writing snack provider. Thanks for knowing that the 'not all' is silent and for always supporting and celebrating me.

To all the men I ever dated/chatted to/got ghosted by on dating apps – I unironically thank you for being pricks. Same goes for my exes (not all of them were pricks, to be fair).

To Girl Gang Manchester for being a community of absolute babes and giving me spaces to explore my new-found Tinder Translator voice.

To my wonderful friends, who have been there for me in many ways, one of which is watching me grow this unexpected thing and cheering me on as it did. Jeyda, Megan, Robyn, Laura, Jo: you are real ones and I love you.

To anyone who has flipped to the acknowledgements hoping to find their name and not found it, I'm sorry. But clearly, I hate you.

That was sarcasm.

Published in 2022 by Hardie Grant Books,
an imprint of Hardie Grant Publishing

Hardie Grant Books (Melbourne)
Wurundjeri Country
Building 1, 658 Church Street
Richmond, Victoria 3121

Hardie Grant Books (London)
5th & 6th Floors
52–54 Southwark Street
London SE1 1UN

hardiegrantbooks.com

Hardie Grant acknowledges the Traditional Owners of the country on which
we work, the Wurundjeri people of the Kulin nation and the Gadigal people of the
Eora nation, and recognises their continuing connection to the land, waters and culture.
We pay our respects to their Elders past and present.

All rights reserved. No part of this publication may be reproduced, stored in a
retrieval system or transmitted in any form by any means, electronic, mechanical,
photocopying, recording or otherwise, without the prior written permission
of the publishers and copyright holders.

The moral rights of the author have been asserted.

Copyright text © Aileen Barratt 2022
Copyright design © Hardie Grant Publishing 2022

 A catalogue record for this
book is available from the
NATIONAL
LIBRARY
OF AUSTRALIA National Library of Australia

Tinder Translator
ISBN 978 1 74379 852 2

10 9 8 7 6 5 4 3 2 1

Commissioning Editor: Alice Hardie-Grant
Project Editor: Emily Hart
Editor: Rochelle Fernandez
Design Manager: Kristin Thomas
Designer: Alissa Dinallo
Typesetting: Hannah Schubert
Production Manager: Todd Rechner
Production Coordinator: Jessica Harvie

Colour reproduction by Splitting Image Colour Studio
Printed in China by Leo Paper Products LTD.

 MIX
Paper from
responsible sources
FSC
www.fsc.org FSC® C020056

The paper this book is printed on is from FSC® certified forests and other
sources. FSC® promotes environmentally responsible, socially beneficial
and economically viable management of the world's forests.